ESOL
for Scottish Qualifications

WORKBOOK

David Maule

SQA Endorsed

HODDER GIBSON

This material has been endorsed by SQA and offers support for the SQA qualifications. SQA endorsement does not mean that this material is essential to achieve any SQA qualification, nor does it mean that this is the only suitable material available to support any SQA qualification. No endorsed material will be used verbatim in setting any SQA examination and any resource lists produced by SQA shall include this and other appropriate texts. While this material has been through an SQA quality assurance process, all responsibility for the content remains with the publisher. Copies of official specifications for all SQA qualifications may be found on the SQA website – www.SQA.org.uk

The Publishers would like to thank the following for permission to reproduce copyright material:

Photo credits
Page 4 (car) © Porsche, courtesy of Porsche Cars Great Britain; Page 6 (beach) © Photodisc/Getty Images, (footballer) © Arthur Kwiatkowski/ istockphoto.com; page 7 (pilot) © Transtock Inc./Alamy; page 16 (ship) © dbphots/Alamy, (airport) © Rex Features; page 18 (restaurant) © Alistair Berg/Digital Vision/ Getty Images, (girls talking) © Datacraft/imagenavi/Getty Images, (business meeting) © Photodisc/Getty Images, (man on train) © David Sacks/ The Image Bank /Getty Images, (woman in street) © www.purestockX.com; page 22 (lottery win) © Monkey Business Images Ltd/Stockbroker/ Photolibrary.com, (two men) © Radius Images/Photolibrary.com; page 23 (overweight man) © Russell Underwood/UpperCut Images/Getty Images, (unicyclist) © James Nesterwitz/Alamy; page 32 (Glasgow) © Mary Evans Picture Library; page 35 (footballer) © Image Source Black/Alamy; page 36 (cloud) © Photodisc/Getty Images, (girl on wall) © Jakob Helbig/Riser/Getty Images, (waiter) © Nick Ayliffe/Alamy, (man running) © Jupiter Images/ Polka Dot/Alamy; page 43 © Alex Segre/Alamy; page 46 (doctor's reception) © Klaus Rose/Das Fotoarchiv/Doc-Stock/Photolibrary.com, (office PA) © Kablonk/Photolibrary.com; page 47 (all musical instruments) © Photodisc/Getty Images; page 52 (soldier) © Maria Olsson/Nordic Photos /Getty Images, (midwife) © Polka Dot Images/Photolibrary.com, (au pair) © Jupiter Images/Pixland/Alamy, (pilot) © Transtock Inc./Alamy, (househusband) © Yellow Dog Productions/Taxi/Getty Images; page 55 © NHS Smokefree

All other photos © Hodder Education.

Acknowledgements
The author would like to thank staff and students of Community-based ESOL at Stevenson College Edinburgh for their help in developing this material and for agreeing to act as photographic subjects. Special thanks are due to Margaret Morgan for her help with Unit 1 and to Ann Morgan Thomas for her support throughout the writing process. Heather Falconer, who edited the text, deserves credit both for this and for her calming influence.

Every effort has been made to trace all copyright holders, but if any have been inadvertently overlooked the Publishers will be pleased to make the necessary arrangements at the first opportunity.

Although every effort has been made to ensure that website addresses are correct at time of going to press, Hodder Gibson cannot be held responsible for the content of any website mentioned in this book. It is sometimes possible to find a relocated web page by typing in the address of the home page for a website in the URL window of your browser.

Hachette's policy is to use papers that are natural, renewable and recyclable products and made from wood grown in sustainable forests. The logging and manufacturing processes are expected to conform to the environmental regulations of the country of origin.

Orders: please contact Bookpoint Ltd, 130 Milton Park, Abingdon, Oxon OX14 4SB. Telephone: (44) 01235 827720. Fax: (44) 01235 400454. Lines are open 9.00 – 5.00, Monday to Saturday, with a 24-hour message answering service. Visit our website at www.hoddereducation.co.uk. Hodder Gibson can be contacted direct on: Tel: 0141 848 1609; Fax: 0141 889 6315; email: hoddergibson@hodder.co.uk

© David Maule 2009
First published in 2009 by
Hodder Gibson, an imprint of Hodder Education,
An Hachette UK Company,
2a Christie Street
Paisley PA1 1NB

Impression number 5 4 3 2 1
Year 2013 2012 2011 2010 2009

All rights reserved. Apart from any use permitted under UK copyright law, no part of this publication may be reproduced or transmitted in any form or by any means, electronic or mechanical, including photocopying and recording, or held within any information storage and retrieval system, without permission in writing from the publisher or under licence from the Copyright Licensing Agency Limited. Further details of such licences (for reprographic reproduction) may be obtained from the Copyright Licensing Agency Limited, Saffron House, 6-10 Kirby Street, London EC1N 8TS.

Cover photo by David Maule. Model: Maryam Zargaran.
Illustrations by Tony Wilkins Design and DC Graphic Design Ltd
Typeset in TradeGothic Light 10.5pt by DC Graphic Design Limited, Swanley Village, Kent
Printed in Great Britain by Hobbs the Printers, Totton, Hants.

A catalogue record for this title is available from the British Library

ISBN-13: 978 0340 971 390

Contents

The English Verb Tenses iv

Introduction
    Unit 1 1

Module 1 Transactional English
    Unit 2   Goods and Services 5
    Unit 3   Health 12
    Unit 4   Travel 15
    Unit 5   Food and Accommodation 18
    Unit 6   Entertainment 22

Module 2 Everyday Communication
    Unit 7   Personal Identity 26
    Unit 8   Daily Life 30
    Unit 9   Physical Environment 34
    Unit 10   Social Environment 39
    Unit 11   Free Time 45

Module 3 Work and Study
    Unit 12   Finding Work 49
    Unit 13   At Work 54
    Unit 14   About Work 58
    Unit 15   Joining a Course 63
    Unit 16   Studying 68

Answers 71

The English Verb Tenses

	past tenses	**present tenses**
simple	Each verb has three parts. For regular verbs, parts 2 and 3 end in **–ed**. Irregular verbs are different. **I drove** We use the past simple for real events in past time: *I went there yesterday*, and for unreal events in present or future time: *If I saw him I'd tell you./ I wish I knew.*	The present simple is just the basic verb. We add **–s** for *he/she/it*. **I drive** The present simple has no meaning. We can use it for different types of action: long-time: *The sun rises in the east.* regular: *I often eat there.* instant: *And he scores for United!* The meanings come from the sentences and situations.
continuous	Add **was/were** and **–ing** to make the past continuous. **I was driving** We use the past continuous to make short actions longer: *He left/was leaving when I arrived*, or longer actions shorter: *She was living in Warsaw when I met her.*	Add **am/is/are** and **-ing** to make the present continuous. **I am driving** We use the present continuous for actions that take some time but are still limited. These can be short-time: *I'm having lunch*, or longer time but still limited: *I'm working too hard these days.*
perfect	Add **had** and change the verb to part 3 to make the past perfect. **I had driven** We use the past perfect to move an action to an earlier time in the past. Compare: *He left when I arrived* with, *He'd left when I arrived*. We also use it for unreal actions in past time: *If I'd known I'd have told you. / I wish I'd known.*	Add **have/has** and change the verb to part 3 to make the present perfect. **I have driven** We use the present perfect: for actions that started in the past and continue up to now: *I've lived here for years.* for actions at an indefinite time in the past: *I've seen that film.* or very recent actions: *He's (just) gone home.*
perfect continuous	Add **had + been + -ing** to make the past perfect continuous. **I had been driving** We use the past perfect continuous: for repeated actions before a time in the past: *I'd been studying a lot for the exam.* for longer actions before a time in the past: *They'd been having a meeting.*	Add **have/has + been + -ing** to make the present perfect continuous. **I have been driving** We use the present perfect continuous: for repeated actions before now: *I've been studying a lot recently.* for longer actions before now: *They've been having a meeting.*

UNIT 1
Introduction

1 have/has got

Write a form of **has/have got** in each space. Watch out for questions and negatives.

1 'What's her dad like?' 'Well, he's big and _____ a black moustache.'
2 '_____ a light?' 'No, sorry, I don't smoke.'
3 Alison's very lonely. _____ any friends.
4 He's rich. _____ millions of pounds and four houses.
5 'How are Ann and Mitch?' 'They're OK – _____ a new car.'
6 Drive faster. _____ ten minutes to get to the station.
7 You are so rude. _____ any manners at all?
8 It's a new car but _____ a very good engine.

2 have/has got haven't/hasn't got

Write **'ve/have got**, **haven't got**, **'s/has got** or **hasn't got** in each space.

1 Maria _____ a new boyfriend. He's very nice.
2 Lennie _____ a job. He's very lonely.
3 I can't go out tonight. I _____ any money.
4 I _____ a new jacket. It didn't cost much.
5 They _____ a computer so they can't use the internet.
6 You won't pass the exam. You _____ a chance.
7 My cat _____ four kittens – she's got five.
8 Hurry up – we _____ much time.
9 She _____ a new scooter. It's a Lambretta.
10 We _____ about five minutes to get to the station.

3 have/has got haven't/hasn't got

Complete the sentences below using the correct form of **have(n't)/has(n't) got** in each space.

Marisol <u>Have you got</u> any brothers or sisters?
Temel Yes, **1** _____ two sisters. How about you?
Marisol Well, **2** _____ two brothers – but **3** _____ any sisters.
Temel What are your brothers' names?
Marisol Carlos and Marcos. They're both older. Marcos is a singer – a good one. He's married to a girl called Filipa. **4** _____ a big house in Rio. **5** _____ six bedrooms. What are your sisters' names?
Temel Ekin and Emel. Ekin's at university in Ankara. **6** _____ a new boyfriend. He's a doctor. **7** _____ a big new flat and a car.
Marisol Do you like him?
Temel Not much. **8** _____ a sense of humour. He's very boring.
Marisol What about the other one?
Temel Emel – she's still at school. She's very musical. **9** _____ a guitar.
Marisol Just like my brother.
Temel Yes, but she hasn't got a very good salary. Nobody in my family **10** _____ much money.

UNIT 1 Introduction

4 Alphabetical order

Look at the word **CHINA** in the box below. Each letter is between two other letters in alphabetical order. Find the other countries.

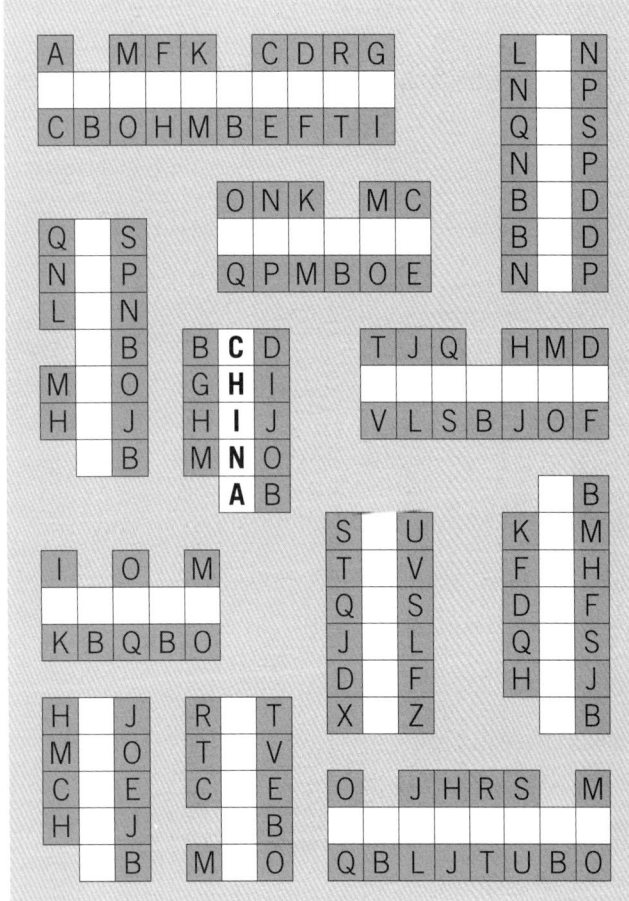

5 Numbers

Vocabulary

In words, write the answers to these sums.

1 the number of days in a fortnight _____

2 a dozen plus one _____

3 the number of players in a football team _____

4 three times five _____

5 the number of months in the year _____

6 the numbers of days in September _____

7 the number of days in a week, plus one _____

8 twenty minus two _____

6 Nationalities

Vocabulary

a Write the nationality for each country in the box on one of the lines below. The first one is done for you.

> Chile   China   Finland   Germany
> Guinea   Hungary   Iran   ~~Iraq~~   Japan
> Korea   Kuwait   Mexico   Pakistan
> Portugal   Russia   Scotland   Sweden
> United States

ending in **-i**	ending in **-ish**	ending in **-ese**
Iraqi		

ending in **-an**	ending in **-ian**	ending in **-ean**

Introduction UNIT 1

b Now write these nationalities. Each one is different. Use a dictionary if you need one.

Country	Nationality
Cyprus	
France	
Greece	
Holland	
Switzerland	

7 Dictionary practice

a Each word below is a noun and a verb, but these have very different meanings – and some have more than one meaning. Use your dictionary and learn the meaning for each form. Then write one sentence for a noun meaning and one for a verb meaning.

desert	noun _____
	verb _____
lead	noun _____
	verb _____
object	noun _____
	verb _____
present	noun _____
	verb _____
rock	noun _____
	verb _____
row	noun _____
	verb _____
tear	noun _____
	verb _____
wind	noun _____
	verb _____

b Only one of these words **always** has the same pronunciation as a noun and a verb. Which is it? Write it here: _____

8 Classroom technology

Vocabulary

You may have some or all of these things in your classroom. What are their names? Write the missing letters.

1 _F_ __ __ __
   _C_ __ __ __ __

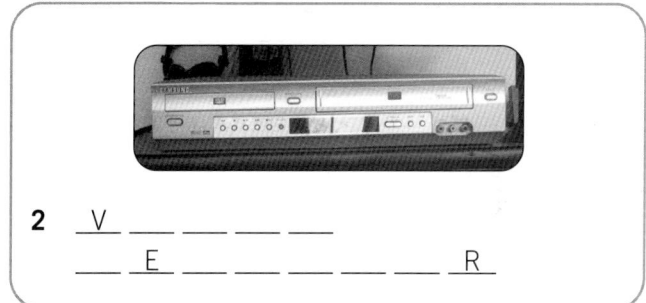

2 _V_ __ __ __ __
   __ _E_ __ __ __ __ __ _R_

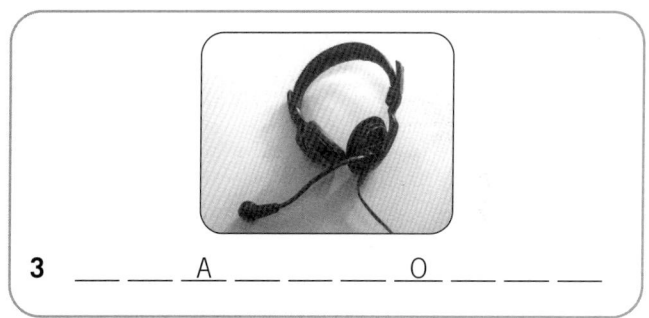

3 __ __ _A_ __ __ _O_ __ __ __

4 __ __ __ _P_ __ __ __ _E_ __

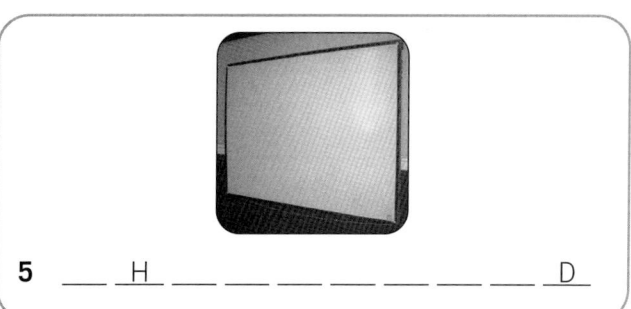

5 __ _H_ __ __ __ __ __ __ __ _D_

UNIT 1 Introduction

6 P _ _ _ _ _ P _ _ _ _ _
   P _ _ _ _ _ _ _ _

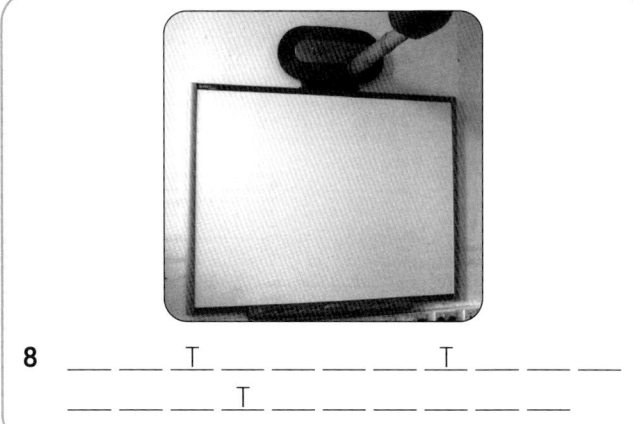

8 _ _ T _ _ _ _ _ T _ _ _
   _ _ _ T _ _ _ _ _

7 _ _ _ _ _ _ Y _ _

9 Writing

What do you want to buy? Write the names of three things you want.

___

Now write about why you want them.

UNIT 2

Goods and Services

1 Present simple: 3rd person *s*

Core grammar

Write the correct form of the verb on each line.

1. Rahal (**have**) _____ a big family.
2. She (**wash**) _____ her clothes at the launderette.
3. Lenka (**miss**) _____ home sometimes.
4. His brother (**teach**) _____ maths.
5. Mike really (**enjoy**) _____ football.
6. My aunt (**fly**) _____ to Canada about three times a year.
7. Hans (**watch**) _____ a lot of TV.
8. Imran (**go**) _____ to the mosque on Fridays.
9. Mahmoud (**argue**) _____ with his mother a lot.
10. Their baby sometimes (**cry**) _____ all night.
11. Magda (**be**) _____ happy in Edinburgh.
12. Huang (**catch**) _____ the 7.00 train to Glasgow every morning.
13. She (**finish**) _____ work at lunchtime on Fridays.
14. She sometimes (**worry**) _____ about her parents.
15. Ahmed (**try**) _____ but he isn't good at maths.

2 Present simple: negatives

Core grammar

Make these sentences negative. The first one is done for you.

> I hate wet weather.
> _I don't hate wet weather_

1. Her parents live far away.
   _____
2. Hannah eats meat.
   _____
3. These trousers are too big for me.
   _____
4. Mark walks to work.
   _____
5. I want a new bike.
   _____
6. My sister usually gets up early.
   _____
7. Karen's a good guitarist.
   _____
8. Mary and her boyfriend like that café.
   _____
9. My dog eats too much.
   _____
10. They make good food in this restaurant.
    _____

3 Present simple: *yes/no* questions

Core grammar

Make questions from these statements. The first one is done for you.

> Abe has got a new bike.
> _Has Abe got a new bike?_ or
> _Does Abe have a new bike?_

1. Elena lives in that house.
   _____
2. You need an ambulance now.
   _____
3. Dave's sorry about the mess.
   _____
4. They have this jacket in blue.
   _____
5. Josep drinks tea.
   _____

UNIT 2 Goods and Services

6 Ana's here now. _____

7 Marta plays tennis on Saturdays.
   _____

8 Alessandra wants more money.
   _____

9 Nasreen and Sandra often go shopping together.
   _____

10 Jan's in London today.
   _____

4 Present simple: wh- questions
Core grammar

Kathrin works in a clothes shop and enjoys her job. Ask her some questions.

Ask her

    how she is today. *How are you today?*

1 where she lives. _____

2 how she gets to work. _____

3 when she starts work. _____

4 how much she earns. _____

5 why she likes her job. _____

6 who she likes in the shop. _____

7 which day of the week she likes best.
   _____

5 Present simple: short answers
Core grammar

Quiz

Answer these questions using forms like **Yes, she does/No, they don't,** etc.

1 Do the Japanese drive on the left?
   ___, ___ ___

2 Does March come after April?
   ___, ___ ___

3 Do penguins live in the Arctic?
   ___, ___ ___

4 Does the French president live in the White House?
   ___, ___ ___

5 Do British people like fried food?
   ___, ___ ___

6 Does Mr Bean live in Italy?
   ___, ___ ___

7 Does it rain a lot in Britain?
   ___, ___ ___

8 Does Scotland have more people than China?
   ___, ___ ___

6 Present simple: habits
Core grammar

Complete the sentences below using the verb at the start. The first one is done for you.

What does Craig do on Saturday mornings?

shop *He shops.*

1 What do Trevor and Jo do on holiday

   sunbathe _____
   on the beach.

2 What does Ivan do on Saturday mornings?

   play _____
   football.

3 What does Clara do at weekends?

   walk _____
   in the hills.

Goods and Services — UNIT 2

4 What does Osman do on Sunday afternoons?

swim _____ in the pool.

5 What does Nada do in the winter?

ski _____ in Italy.

6 What does Trevor do in the evening?

play _____ the piano.

7 What does Kate do for a living?

teach _____ in the college.

8 What does Alison do most days?

fly _____ a plane.

7 Present continuous: spelling the –ing form

Core grammar

Write the -ing form of the verbs below. The first three are done for you.

1	like *liking*	8	bite	_____
2	put *putting*	9	take	_____
3	die *dying*	10	sit	_____
4	come _____	11	choose	_____
5	swim _____	12	get	_____
6	study _____	13	save	_____
7	move _____	14	begin	_____

15	write _____	23	carry	_____
16	dig _____	24	have	_____
17	care _____	25	change	_____
18	open _____	26	run	_____
19	arrive _____	27	cry	_____
20	hide _____	28	play	_____
21	meet _____	29	drive	_____
22	ride _____	30	like	_____

8 Present continuous: statements

Core grammar

Change the verbs in these sentences to the **present continuous** and write them on the lines.

1 My mum (**come**) _____ to have lunch with us.

2 It's a hot day and many people (**swim**) _____ in the sea here.

3 He (**sit**) _____ at his desk but I think he's asleep.

4 The people next door (**move**) _____ to a new house.

5 The weather (**change**) _____ – I think we can go out.

6 Where's Jenny? She (**run**) _____ around the park.

7 The team's playing well – we (**win**) _____ the game.

8 Wait a minute – I (**open**) _____ some tins of tomatoes.

9 I'm not going out – I (**save**) _____ money for my holiday.

10 Give these plants some water – they (**die**) _____ .

UNIT 2 Goods and Services

9 Present continuous: positive, negative and questions

Core grammar

Read this phone conversation between Maria and Justin. Write the verbs in the present continuous, in the positive, negative or question form.

Justin Hi, Maria. How are you?

Maria Oh, hi Justin. I'm fine. Where are you?

Justin I (**sit**) _____ in a café. Mehmet's with me. I (**drink**) _____ coffee and he (**eat**) _____ , as usual.

Maria Well, that's nice.

Justin What about you? (**You study**) _____ ?

Maria I (**not work**) _____ right now. In fact, I (**sit**) _____ in the front room.

Justin (**You watch**) _____ the football?

Maria Yes, it's a good game.

Justin It's great – and United (**win**) _____ .

Maria How do you know?

Justin It's on TV in the café here. We're in Dario's. It's not far away. Come and have a coffee.

Maria Oh, Justin, I (**write**) _____ my essay this afternoon.

Justin Do it tonight. It's great here – everybody* (**enjoy**) _____ the game.

Maria No, I (**not go**) _____ out today. I'm too busy.

Justin You (**work**) _____ too hard. OK, see you.

Maria Bye, Justin.

*note that **everybody** is singular.

10 Present continuous: questions and short answers

Core grammar

Write a question in the present continuous on each line on the left. Then use one of the forms in the box to answer it on the right.

| am | 'm not | are | aren't | is | isn't |

1 sleep ' _Is he sleeping?_ ' 'Yes, he _is_ .'
2 rain ' _it_ _____ ' 'No, it _____ .'
3 laugh ' _____ ' 'No, I' _____ .'
4 watch ' _____ ' 'Yes, they _____ .'
5 work ' _____ ' 'Yes, I _____ .'
6 dream ' _____ ' 'No, you _____ .'
7 come ' _____ ' 'No, we _____ .'
8 grow ' _____ ' 'Yes, it _____ .'
9 sing ' _____ ' 'Yes, she _____ .'
10 lie ' _____ ' 'No, he _____ .'
11 talk ' _____ ' 'No, she _____ .'
12 shop ' _____ ' 'Yes, we _____ .'
13 eat ' _____ ' 'Yes, they _____ .'
14 go ' _____ ' 'No, they _____ .'

11 Present simple or present continuous

Core grammar

Choose the correct answer. Tick one of the boxes.

1 You look tired.
  ☐ **A** Yes – I study for the exam next week.
  ☐ **B** Yes – I'm studying for the exam next week.

2 Where's Mr Anders?
  ☐ **A** He flies from London. Maybe his plane's late.
  ☐ **B** He's flying from London. Maybe his plane's late.

Goods and Services UNIT 2

3 What do you do?
- [ ] A I'm a plumber.
- [ ] B I'm turning off the water.

4 What's Sacha doing?
- [ ] A He's an actor.
- [ ] B He's having a bath.

5 Tell me about your brother.
- [ ] A He's a teacher. He is live in London.
- [ ] B He's a teacher. He lives in London.

6 Are you busy?
- [ ] A Not really – I'm just read the paper.
- [ ] B Not really – I'm just reading the paper.

7 I didn't know you liked running.
- [ ] A I don't but I do it for a few weeks to lose some weight.
- [ ] B I don't but I'm doing it for a few weeks to lose some weight.

8 And what about your grandfather?
- [ ] A Well, he was born in Lahore and he still lives there.
- [ ] B Well, he was born in Lahore and he's still living there.

9 What do you know about Cairo?
- [ ] A It's the capital of Egypt. It stands on the River Nile.
- [ ] B It's the capital of Egypt. It's standing on the River Nile.

10 Why are you annoyed with me?
- [ ] A Because this is a difficult situation and you're not serious.
- [ ] B Because this is a difficult situation and you're not being serious.

12 Present continuous: *always*

Grammar extension

Choose between the present simple with **always** (= *always*) or the present continuous with **always** (= *often*) in these sentences.

1 The sun **always rises/is always rising** in the east – that's the way the world works.

2 My brother **always gets/is always getting** hurt playing rugby.

3 When mum comes to visit us we **always take/'re always taking** her out for lunch.

4 I have to go to London quite often and I **always take/'m always taking** the train.

5 I **always meet/'m always meeting** Sanjeev in the shopping centre.

6 Reg travels to some away matches and he **always watches/'s always watching** the team when they play at home.

7 People **always get/are always getting** shot in America.

8 Gran **always buys/'s always buying** the kids little presents.

9 I **always go/I'm always going** to see my aunt when I'm in Perth.

13 Plurals

Core grammar

Write the plural of one of the words in the box on each of the lines below.

> bus   church   deer   hero   knife   lady
> loaf   mouse   party   potato

1 I can't cut the tomatoes – all of the _____ are blunt. _____

2 In the Highlands you sometimes see _____ up on the hills.

3 We've got _____ in the house – I need to buy a trap.

4 Many of the old _____ in Scotland are now flats or shops.

5 Two _____ go there – the 24 and the 41. The 24 is quicker.

6 We need some bread – get two _____ , will you?

7 All the _____ wear expensive hats for the garden party.

8 You're tired – you're going to too many _____ .

9 These are new _____ – you don't need to peel them.

10 All of his _____ are footballers – he never thinks about anybody else.

9

UNIT 2 Goods and Services

14 Plurals: nouns with no singular

Grammar extension

Write an appropriate word on each line.

1 'Can I help you?' 'Yes, I'm looking for a _____ of jeans.'

2 There's a police _____ at the door. He wants to speak to you.

3 These scissors _____ too much – find a cheaper pair.

4 He lost his job last week but he has _____ savings so he'll be OK for a while.

5 There are three _____ of stairs in the house and they all need painting.

6 Funds are very low now. We have to make some _____ soon.

7 The barracks are a large _____ on the west side of the castle.

8 The odds against that horse _____ 100 to 1.

15 Prepositions of place

Core grammar

Read the quotations below. Write one preposition from the box on each line.

> above   behind   beside   between
> in front of   under

1 'There is only one difference _____ a madman and me. I am not mad.'
  Salvador Dali (1904 – 1989)

2 'There is nothing new _____ the sun but there are lots of old things we don't know.'
  Ambrose Bierce (1842 – 1914)

3 'Reality is something you rise _____ .'
  Liza Minnelli (1946 –)

4 'Don't walk _____ me, I may not follow. Don't walk _____ me, I may not lead. Walk _____ me and be my friend.'
  Albert Camus (1913 – 1960)

16 Money

Vocabulary

Work with a partner. Write one word or phrase from the box on each line.

> change   cheque   credit card   currency
> receipt   reduced

1 The Euro is the _____ in a number of European countries.

2 I can't give you your money back if you don't have a _____ .

3 Lots of things in the shops are _____ in January.

4 Have you got any _____ ? I want to get some coffee from the machine.

5 Your _____ is in the post. You'll get it tomorrow.

6 I paid for the holiday with my _____ so I need to find some money soon.

17 Buying things

Vocabulary

Decide which sentence, **1-6** goes with each sentence **a-f**.

1 Oh no – my purse is empty again.

2 You can pay a deposit today.

3 This jumper's too expensive.

4 There's a mistake in the bill.

5 Wait till after Christmas.

6 This jacket's too tight.

a Look for a cheaper one.

b I'll have to use my credit card.

c We can buy things in the sales.

d We only had two coffees – not three.

e I'll take it back and ask for a bigger one.

f Then you pay the rest in monthly instalments.

18 Writing

You receive this voucher from a department store –

James Bewis Stores

08456 085 909

Congratulations!

You are the winner of our customer prize draw!

With this voucher you can spend **£250** in any of our stores.

Choose anything you like up from any of our departments:	
Home & Garden	Fashion
Electrical Appliances	Womenswear
Technology	Bedroom
Televisions	Kitchen
Books/DVDs	Food and Drink

- Write an email to a friend.
- Invite them to come shopping with you.
- Write about what you want to buy, and why.

○ Send

To:
Subject:

19 Sound and spelling

Pronunciation

Some of these pairs of words end in the same vowel sound – they rhyme. Others don't. Mark the rhyming words with a tick (✔) and the others with a cross (✘).

1	new	few	_____
2	sew	chew	_____
3	tie	guy	_____
4	high	sigh	_____
5	blow	now	_____
6	toe	shoe	_____
7	day	they	_____
8	so	do	_____
9	toy	boy	_____
10	cough	tough	_____
11	high	pie	_____
12	through	dough	_____

UNIT 3

Health

1 Countable and uncountable nouns

Core grammar

Write one of the forms in the box on each line below.

> some (x2)   any   much (x2)   many
>   a lot of   no

1 Let's go for lunch. How _____ money do you have?

2 Don't buy any butter. We've got _____ it.

3 There are _____ onions in the shop – not one.

4 How _____ milk do you want?

5 Are you hungry? There's still _____ spaghetti here.

6 Is there _____ news about Maria? Is she still in hospital?

7 There are _____ plates here. How many do we need?

8 There are some spoons here but not very _____ .

2 Nouns that are countable and uncountable

Grammar extension

Decide if these nouns are **countable** or **uncountable** or both. Tick one or two boxes.

		countable	uncountable
1	flour	☐	☐
2	wall	☐	☐
3	glass	☐	☐
4	flower	☐	☐
5	paper	☐	☐
6	meat	☐	☐
7	coffee	☐	☐
8	song	☐	☐
9	music	☐	☐
10	pizza	☐	☐

3 Nouns that are countable and uncountable

Grammar extension

Write **a** or **some** on each line.

1 We need _____ glass to fix the broken window.

2 Get me _____ paper while you're out. I want to read about the election.

3 Can you buy _____ football for Jim's birthday?

4 That's a bargain – _____ whole roast chicken for two pounds!

5 Put _____ milk in this sauce – it's too thick.

6 Did you have _____ good time on holiday?

7 I want to watch TV tonight. There's _____ football on.

8 The house is in the country, beside _____ wood.

9 Do you want _____ chicken with your salad?

10 Give me _____ spaghetti – I'm starving.

4 Nouns that are countable and uncountable

Grammar extension

Write the **uncountable** or **plural** form of each noun in brackets on the line

1 Can you buy a couple of _____? I want something to read on the train. *(paper)*

2 I don't like tables made of _____ . Do you have a wooden one? *(glass)*

3 Put about a dozen _____ on that plate and put it on the table. *(cake)*

4 Come on – hurry up. We don't have much _____ . *(time)*

5 He's overweight because he drinks too much _____ . *(beer)*

Health UNIT 3

6 Shazia bought two _____ for the biryani. (chicken)

7 We'll need a few more _____ for the party. (beer)

8 Get me three pieces of _____ about 2 metres long. (wood)

9 I don't want so much _____ – cut me a thinner slice. (cake)

10 OK, can I have three _____ and a hot chocolate? (coffee)

11 There's a small _____ on the hillside behind the house. (wood)

12 How many _____ do I have to tell you? (time)

13 The doctor said I drink too much _____ . (coffee)

14 These _____ are dirty – you'd better wash them again. (glass)

15 There's _____ all over the floor – pick it up. (paper)

16 I'd like some Mexican _____ and sliced peppers on my sandwich. (chicken)

5 Like as a verb or preposition
Core grammar
Write one word one each line to make each pair of sentences mean the same thing.

1 My brother and I are similar.
 = I _____ like my brother.

2 These two cars are almost the same.
 = These two cars _____ quite like each other.

3 London is different from Paris.
 = London _____ like Paris.

4 The new boss isn't popular.
 = They _____ like the new boss.

5 Sadia looks like Nargis.
 = Sadia _____ like Nargis.

6 People in Britain don't eat much garlic.
 = Many people in Britain _____ like garlic.

7 I dislike my uncle Igor.
 = I _____ not like my uncle Igor.

8 Tasneem isn't fond of cooking.
 = Tasneem _____ like cooking.

6 Present simple and present continuous
Grammar extension
Write each verb in bold in either the **present simple** or the **present continuous**.

1 I'm a bit tired because we (**paint**) _____ the living room and it (**take**) _____ a few days.

2 Let's say you (**drive**) _____ to work one day and on the way you (**have**) _____ an accident.

3 'Why (**he shout**) _____ ?' 'I don't know – he's certainly annoyed about something.'

4 Now, in this scene, Peter (**come**) _____ into the room, (**sit**) _____ down and (**start**) _____ to read the paper. Then Doreen _____ (**arrive**)...

5 My mother (**live**) _____ on the other side of town but she (**stay**) _____ with us till my baby arrives.

6 ... so I (**take**) _____ three eggs, (**crack**) _____ them into the bowl and (**stir**) _____ until the mixture's smooth.

7 I (**cycle**) _____ to work until they fix the car.

8 'Dilram's in hospital again – he fell off his motorbike.' 'Yeah? He always (**do**) _____ that.'

7 Medical jobs
Vocabulary
Look at sentences 1-7 below. Decide if they are correct or incorrect. Write a tick (✔) or a cross (✗) on each line.

1 GPs don't work in hospitals. ___

2 Dr Smith is a dentist. ___

3 All patients are in hospitals. ___

4 Nurses always work in hospitals. ___

5 We sometimes call chemists 'pharmacists'. ___

6 All chemists work with medicine and drugs. ___

7 Surgeons don't work in a surgery. ___

UNIT 3 Health

8 Medical problems & treatment

Vocabulary

Match the medical problems in the box with the treatments **1–6**. Write one letter **a–f** on each line.

> **a** flu **b** a broken arm **c** a broken leg
> **d** a cut hand **e** a stiff neck **f** an infected eye

1 'I'll put a bandage on it.' ___
2 'You'll have to see the physiotherapist.' ___
3 'We'll put it in plaster and give you crutches.' ___
4 'Stay warm and drink lots of fluids.' ___
5 'You'll have to use drops and take antibiotics.' ___
6 'We'll put it in a sling.' ___

9 Writing

A local newspaper is running a competition. Read about it below and write your entry.

Scotland is an unhealthy country.

People are overweight. They smoke and drink too much. They eat too much fast food.

What can we do? How can we improve Scotland's health?

Write your ideas here. Send them to the Editor. We'll print the best entry and send you £100

_____
_____
_____
_____
_____
_____
_____

10 Pronunciation

The words in the box have four different stress patterns. Write them on the correct lines below.

> animal annoying control instruction
> instrument mature nature onion
> online petrol recipe recover

●• _____ _____ _____
•● _____ _____ _____
●•• _____ _____ _____
•●• _____ _____ _____

UNIT 4
Travel

1 *a* or *the*

Core grammar

Write **a**, **an**, **the** or nothing on each line below.

1 My brother is _____ architect. He works for _____ City Council.

2 Remember to lock _____ front door when you leave.

3 There's _____ dog in the garden. I think it's from across the street.

4 Rosaria's got _____ brown hair but she dyes it blonde.

5 Jack plays _____ piano and _____ drums.

6 This car's getting old. We need to buy _____ new one.

7 I like that film because of _____ actors in it.

8 What does it say in _____ newspaper?

9 There's _____ Mr Jackson to see you – I don't know him.

10 I'm really tired – I need _____ few days off.

2 *the* with places

Grammar extension

Look at the map. When we write place names on a map, we don't normally use *the*. But when we speak or write, we use *the* with some of them, for example: 'The River Thames is in the south-east of England,' but 'The Aberdeen is in the north-east of Scotland.'

Some of the places on the map need *the* when we speak or write. Tick these boxes.

3 *too*

Core grammar

Choose either **a** or **b** as the better choice to follow **1-7**.

1 It's too hot today a so I'll stay in.
                      b but I'll go out.

2 That car's too expensive a but I'm going to buy it.
                             b and I'm not going to buy it.

3 'You put too much salt in the soup.'
   a 'Yes, but I like it a bit salty.'
   b 'I know – I'm sorry about that.'

4 That horse is too slow. a It can't possibly win.
                            b It might win the race.

5 He's too old for the job a and he should retire.
                             b but he can still do it well.

UNIT 4 Travel

6 This test is too difficult   a but I'll finish it.
                                               b – I can't finish it.

7 He's too clever, really. a He can't easily talk to other people.
                                           b I really admire him.

4 very and too

Core grammar

Choose between **very** and **too** in these sentences.

1 A present for me? That's **very/too** nice of you.

2 Tom's cycling to work these days and he says he feels **very/too** fit now.

3 That computer's **very/too** expensive. We can't afford it.

4 She drives down the motorway at 100 miles an hour. That's **very/too** fast – she'll get a speeding ticket.

5 It's **very/too** cold today but I'm still going out for a walk.

6 We're moving to another house. This one's **very/too** far away from my new job.

7 She's a **very/too** clever student – she wants to be an architect.

8 They're giving me **very/too** much work to do. I'm going to get a new job.

5 Travel

Vocabulary

Three people are travelling and are making calls from their mobile phones. Write one word from the box on each line.

> buffet   cabin   carriage   check-in desk
> deck   excess baggage   flight
> gangway   hand luggage   harbour
> luggage   platform   station

1 Hi Tomas. I'm on the ship now, in Southampton _____. The _____'s up and they're getting ready to leave. My _____'s on the top _____ and it's quite nice.

2 Hi, I'm at the _____ now. My train's in and I'm walking along the _____ to my _____. This train doesn't have a _____ so I've got some sandwiches.

3 It's me, love. I'm standing in the queue at the _____. I'm a little worried because my _____ leaves in fifty minutes. Also, I've got a lot of _____ with me and I might have to pay _____. Maybe I can take the smallest suitcase onto the plane as _____.

*In Britain, the US word **baggage** is used for **luggage** on flights.

6 Road signs

Vocabulary

Choose one meaning from the box for each sign.

> Mini roundabout   Minimum speed
> No motor vehicles   No right turn
> No stopping   No U-turns   One way traffic
> Road narrows on the right
> Vehicles may pass on either side   Wild animals

a _____   b _____   c _____

d _____   e _____   f _____

g _____   h _____   i _____   j _____

Travel UNIT 4

7 Writing

You receive this email from a friend:

○ Send

To:
Subject:

Hi,

You know I have a week's holiday next month. Well, I really need a break. I want to go away somewhere. Can you come with me? I know you have your holidays at the same time. But where can we go? I don't know – I'm so bad at decisions. Do you have any ideas? Write back and tell me.

Cheers,

Write a reply. Say you want to go on holiday with your friend. Give some ideas about where to go. Write about different kinds of holidays.

8 *a* or *an*

Pronunciation:

- Choose between **a** or **an** for each abbreviation.
- Find the meanings of the abbreviations then write them on the lines after **a** or **an**.
- Underline the ones that have **an** before the abbreviation but **a** before the full form – or the other way round.

1 **a/an** BA graduate _____

2 **a/an** CIA agent _____

3 **a/an** ESOL student _____

4 **a/an** IOU _____

5 **a/an** JP _____

6 **a/an** MP _____

7 **a/an** NHS hospital _____

8 **a/an** SQA assessment _____

9 **a/an** UN conference _____

10 **a/an** WHO report _____

17

UNIT 5

Food and Accommodation

1 Do you like ..?/Would you like ..?

Core grammar

Tick ✔ the correct form for each conversation.

1 ☐ Do you like soup?
   Yes – it smells good.
   ☐ Would you like some soup?

2 ☐ Do you like basketball?
   No, I prefer football.
   ☐ Would you like to play basketball?

3 ☐ Do you like films?
   Yes, I watch a lot of them.
   ☐ Would you like to watch a film?

4 ☐ Do you like sweets?
   No thanks.
   ☐ Would you like some sweets?

5 ☐ Do you like shopping?
   No – I hate it.
   ☐ Would you like to go shopping?

6 ☐ Do you like dogs?
   No, there isn't room in my flat.
   ☐ Would you like to have a dog?

2 Do you like ..?/Would you like ..?

Core grammar

Answer these questions about yourself. Use Yes, I do.
Yes, I would.
No, I don't.
No, I wouldn't.

1 Would you like to be rich? _____

2 Do you like cats? _____

3 Would you like to go out tonight? _____

4 Would you like to be a famous singer? _____

5 Do you like coffee? _____

6 Would you like to go to China? _____

7 Do you like computers? _____

8 Would you like a new computer? _____

3 'll or (be) going to: intention

Core grammar

Look at the dialogues below. Change the verbs in brackets to their **'ll** or **(be) going to** form.

1 'Would you like to order, sir?' 'Yes, wait a minute. OK, I (have) the fish.'

_____

2 'Emma looks happy today.' 'I hope so. She (get married) on Saturday.'

_____

3 'Somebody has to go to Manchester – today! There are big problems in the office.' 'OK, I (go).'

_____

4 'The train gets in at ten past eleven.' 'Ten past? OK, I (meet) you at the station.'

_____

5 'Anna, can Jake and you meet me at 11 tomorrow?' 'I'm OK, but Jake (fly) to Paris tonight.'

_____

Food and Accommodation UNIT 5

4 'll or (be) going to: intention
Core grammar
Read each situation below. Choose sentence **a** or **b** and tick one of the boxes.

1 Your friend is sitting her driving test tomorrow. You know that she's a good driver. She's a little nervous and you want to help her relax. What do you say:

   a Don't worry – you'll pass. ☐
   b Don't worry – you're going to pass. ☐

2 You're watching a football match. Your team is 3–1 down with ten minutes to go, and they're looking very tired. What do you say to your friend?

   a I think we'll lose this one. ☐
   b I think we're going to lose this one. ☐

3 You're in an Indian restaurant. Your friend wants to order a really hot curry and suggests you have one too. You don't really like hot curry. What do you say?

   a No thanks – I don't think I'll enjoy it. ☐
   b No thanks – I don't think I'm going to enjoy it. ☐

4 Your cousin is going to France for a holiday. She's staying at a campsite. You stayed in the same place last year. What do you say?

   a It's really nice – you'll like it. ☐
   b It's really nice – you're going to like it. ☐

5 You're at a business meeting. A new project is six months behind schedule, its costs are rising and the project director has just resigned. The boss asks you what you think of the project.

   a I don't think it will work – let's cancel it. ☐
   b I don't think it's going to work – let's cancel it. ☐

6 You're starting a course at a university away from home. You have a place in a flat with students that you don't know. Your family think you might not enjoy this. What do you say?

   a It's OK – I'll be fine. ☐
   b It's OK – I'm going to be fine. ☐

5 would rather/would prefer
Grammar extension
Tick (✔) the correct forms below.

1 Shall we have a coffee? ___
   I'd prefer have tea. ___

   Shall we to have a coffee? ___
   I'd prefer tea. ___

2 Let's going out tonight. ___
   I'd rather stay in. ___

   Let's go out tonight. ___
   I'd rather to stay in. ___

3 Let's have lunch. ___
   I'm not hungry. I'd rather waiting. ___

   Let's having lunch. ___
   I'm not hungry. I'd rather wait. ___

   OK – in about an hour?
   Yes, I'd prefer to that. ___
   Yes, I'd prefer that. ___

4 Shall we watch a video? ___
   I'd prefer not to. ___

   Shall we watching a video? ___
   I'd prefer not. ___

5 Would you like a cake? ___
   I'd rather a biscuit. ___

   Would you liking a cake? ___
   I'd rather have a biscuit. ___

6 Food definitions
Vocabulary
Match the words and phrases **1-8** to the foods **a-h**.

1	shellfish	a	gravy
2	uncooked	b	lamb
3	flavouring	c	mince
4	young sheep	d	muesli
5	it covers pies	e	pastry
6	breakfast cereal	f	prawn
7	meat in small pieces	g	raw
8	brown sauce for meat	h	spices

UNIT 5 Food and Accommodation

7 Fruit

Vocabulary

Read this e-mail:

Send

To:
Subject:

Hi – listen, I want to make a fruit salad for the dinner tonight and I don't have much time. Could you buy some fruit on the way home? I'll need some berries – strawberries, or raspberries if they don't have them. And a mango, a melon – honeydew, not watermelon – 2-3 peaches, a couple of pears, some oranges and tangerines. Get me about ½ a kilo of grapes – we need some for the fruit bowl as well. I'll need a pineapple if they have one. If not, get me a tin. Oh, and I'll need a couple of passion fruits. Ta.

Love,

Nicky.

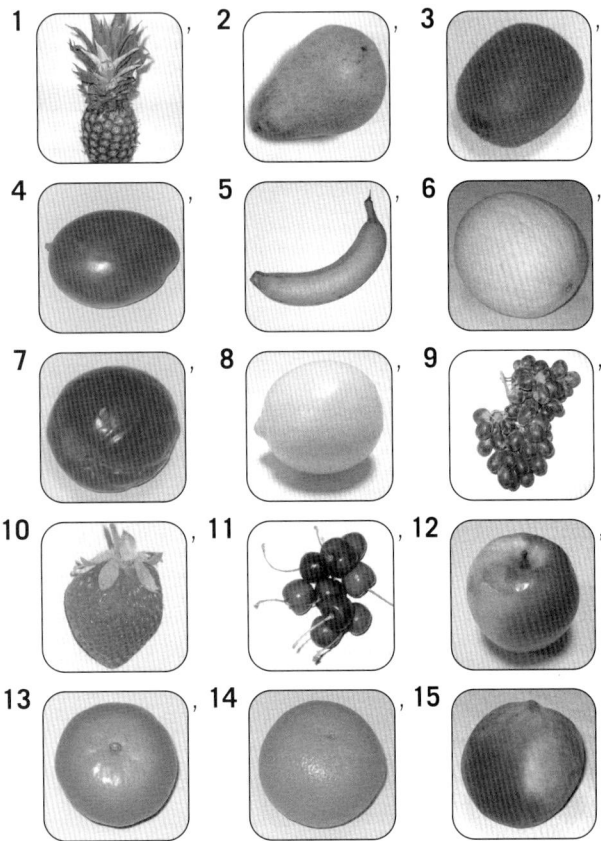

Now write the numbers of the fruit you need on this line:

_____

8 Things to eat

Vocabulary

Look at the pictures below. Write the correct names on the lines 1-7 on the next page.

aubergine   cabbage   carrot   cauliflower

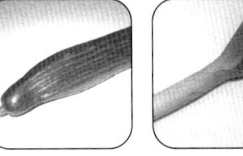
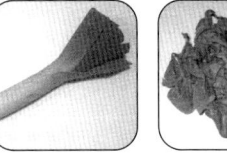

courgette   cucumber   leek   lettuce

mushroom   onion   potato   tomato

sweetcorn

Food and Accommodation UNIT **5**

1 This one's a fruit: _____
2 This one's a fungus: _____
3 These grow under the ground: _____ _____
4 These are made of leaves: _____ _____
5 This can make you cry: _____
6 These are purple: _____
7 This is yellow: _____

9 Writing

Think about a country that you know well. Write an e-mail to a friend. Talk about the food there. Write about these things:

- How is the food different from in Britain?
- What kinds of food can you eat there?
- Is the food people cook at home different from the food in restaurants? If it is, describe the differences.
- What do you like or not like about the food in this country?

Send
To:
Subject:

10 Pronunciation

Add **s** to the start of each word below to make a new word. Write it on the line and make sure you spell it correctly. Then practise saying the word. The first one is done for you.

	key	**s** + key =	ski
1	lamb	**s** + lamb =	_____
2	leap	**s** + leap =	_____
3	leave	**s** + leave =	_____
4	knees	**s** + knees =	_____
5	no	**s** + no =	_____
6	teddy	**s** + teddy =	_____
7	tough	**s** + tough =	_____
8	ton	**s** + ton =	_____
9	tile	**s** + tile =	_____
10	wet	**s** + wet =	_____

UNIT 6

Entertainment

1 Comparative and superlative adjectives

Core grammar

Look at these facts about Cairo, Edinburgh and Karachi. Write the correct form in the box on each line.

> the least   the fewest   less
> more (x2)   the most (x2)   fewer

	population	annual rainfall
Cairo	8,000,000	25mm
Edinburgh	500,000	625mm
Karachi	12,000,000	200mm

1 Cairo has _____ people than Karachi but _____ than Edinburgh.

2 Karachi gets _____ rain than Cairo but _____ than Edinburgh.

3 Of the three, Edinburgh has _____ rain and Cairo has _____.

4 Edinburgh has _____ people and Karachi has _____.

2 Comparative & superlative adjectives

Core grammar

Look at the ages and heights of these three students.

Salima
age: 33
height: 1m 78cms

Fahad
age: 35
height: 1m 78cms

Noriko
age: 35
height: 1m 53cms

Fahad **is as old as** Noriko.
  Fahad **is taller than** Noriko.
    Noriko **isn't as tall as** Salima.

Now make comparisons. Write one word on each line.

1 old   Noriko ___ ___ ___ ___ Fahad.
2 old   Fahad ___ ___ ___ Salima.
3 tall   Noriko ___ ___ ___ Fahad.
4 tall   Fahad ___ ___ ___ Salima.
5 old   Salima ___ ___ ___ Fahad.
6 tall   Salima ___ ___ ___ Noriko.
7 old   Noriko ___ ___ ___ Salima.
8 old   Salima ___ ___ ___ ___ Noriko.
9 tall   Salima ___ ___ ___ ___ Fahad.
10 young   Salima ___ ___ ___.
11 small   Noriko ___ ___ ___.

3 Comparative and superlative adjectives

Core grammar

Finish these sentences. Use the word in bold and any others you need.

1 **lucky**

Joe's not .... his friend.

2 **big**

He's not .... her boyfriend.

Entertainment UNIT 6

3 slim

He's not ....
he wants to be.

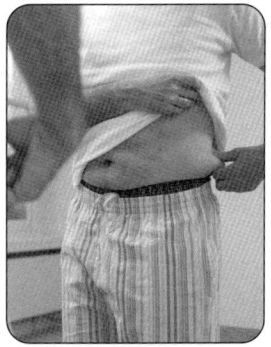

4 difficult

'You know, this isn't
.... it looks.'

4

Craigforth College
Term 2
Monday 9th January – Friday 31st March

finish Term 2 _____ _____ Friday 31st March.

5

... FLIGHT BA 3415 FROM PARIS DUE TO ARRIVE 14.45 ....

arrive The Paris flight _____ _____ 14.45.

6

SALE!
Everything must go!!
Till 15th January

end The sale _____ _____ the 15th January.

4 Present simple for the future

Core grammar

Write a sentence about each notice. Write one word on each line. Use the verb on the left in the **present simple**.

1

CELTIC V ABERDEEN
SATURDAY, APRIL 25,
KICK OFF 12.15PM
Ticket prices:
Adults £25
Concessions (under 16 & 65+) £15

play Celtic _____ Aberdeen _____ Saturday 25th.

2

GLASGOW TO LONDON
Next train :   10:00

leave The next train _____ London _____ _____ 10 o'clock.

3

Ghandi Indian Restaurant
Opening time tonight: 7.00

open The restaurant _____ tonight _____ 7.00.

5 Present continuous for the future

Core grammar

Decide if these sentences are right or wrong. Write a tick (✔) or a cross (✘) on each line.

1 My driving test is tomorrow. I'm passing it. ___

2 I can't see you tonight – I'm going to the cinema. ___

3 We're having fun at the party tomorrow night. ___

4 Do you think Scotland are winning the game on Saturday? ___

5 It's just a short holiday – we're leaving on Friday and coming back the following Tuesday. ___

6 I'm meeting my gran for lunch tomorrow. ___

7 I'm feeling bad now and I think I'm feeling worse tomorrow. ___

8 Is Judy coming to the meeting this afternoon? ___

9 Alexei's starting a new job on Monday. ___

10 He's old and very ill. I think he's dying soon. ___

UNIT 6 Entertainment

6 Present simple or present continuous for the future

Core grammar

Write the verbs in the **present simple** or the **present continuous**. Remember to pay attention to questions and negatives.

1 Susie ………… (**have**) lunch with Marcia tomorrow.
2 We have to go now. The film ………… (**start**) at seven o'clock.
3 I ………… (**not go**) out with Bob tonight. I'm too tired.
4 When ………… her plane ………… (**arrive**)?
5 ………… they ………… (**get**) married soon?
6 The train ………… (**leave**) in an hour.
7 ………… Alice ………… (**go**) to London tomorrow?
8 Slow down – the shops ………… (**not open**) till nine.
9 I have to leave early – I ………… (**see**) the doctor at four.
10 ………… you ………… (**have**) a test on Monday?

7 Present continuous or *(be) going to* for future.

Grammar extension

Each sentence **a** below has the **present continuous** used for the future. Each sentence **b** has **going to**. Sometimes both **a** and **b** are good English sentences. Sometimes only sentence **b** is good. Tick (✔) the box where the sentence is **good**. Put a cross (✘) where it isn't.

1 a Nuria thinks she's doing well at the interview on Friday. ☐
  b Nuria thinks she's going to do well at the interview on Friday. ☐
2 a Lars and I are going out for a meal tonight. ☐
  b Lars and I are going to go out for a meal tonight. ☐
3 a I think one day Matt's winning an Olympic gold medal for swimming. ☐
  b I think one day Matt's going to win an Olympic gold medal for swimming. ☐
4 a Jan says she's being a singer when she grows up. ☐
  b Jan says she's going to be a singer when she grows up. ☐
5 a Doug's wife says he's coming home tomorrow. ☐
  b Doug's wife says he's going to come home tomorrow. ☐
6 a Morgana and Vlad are getting married in August. ☐
  b Morgana and Vlad are are going to get married in August. ☐
7 a I think he's doing something really stupid one of these days. ☐
  b I think he's going to do something really stupid one of these days. ☐
8 a It looks like her grandmother is dying soon. ☐
  b It looks like her grandmother is going to die soon. ☐

8 Entertainment

Vocabulary

Look at the groups of words below. In each group there is a word from another group. Cross out this word and write it in its correct group.

TV	cinema
article	film star
channel	game show
documentary	studio
soap opera	stuntman/woman

theatre	newspaper
extra	column
interval	editor
performance	playwright
stage	reporter

Entertainment UNIT 6

9 Writing

Look at these styles of music:

blues   classical   bhangra   country
folk   garage   heavy metal   house
jazz   pop   raga   rock
reggae   rock   soul   techno

What kind – or kinds – of music do you like?

Do you listen or do you also play an instrument?

How do you listen? To music on TV, DVD, the internet ...

Which instrument(s) do you play?
How good are you?

Who are your favourite singers and musicians?

Write about it here:

10 Pronunciation

Each word below has a silent letter. <u>Underline</u> it.

1 walk
2 autumn
3 knot
4 thumb
5 wrist
6 palm
7 resign
8 sword
9 debt
10 hour
11 ghost
12 castle
13 muscle
14 scientific

UNIT 7

Personal Identity

1 Adjectives and adverbs

Core grammar

One word in each sentence is wrong. Write the correct form on each line.

1 Bowl straightly, will you? You're missing all the pins.
   _____

2 We can't go out – it's raining hardly.
   _____

3 Jo sings very good, doesn't she? _____

4 They'll arrive quite lately – the car broke down.
   _____

5 English is a wide spoken language.
   _____

6 Slow down – you're walking too fastly.
   _____

7 He smiled at me in a friendlily way.
   _____

8 Luke crashed his car. He wasn't hurt, lucky.
   _____

2 Suffixes

Core grammar

Words in English can become different parts of speech when we add a suffix. For example:

walk (verb) + **-er** becomes **walker** (noun)

nation (noun) + **-al** becomes **national** (adjective)

Write the correct words on the lines below. Be careful with the spelling. The ones where spelling changes are marked with an asterisk, e.g. **run*** – **runner**

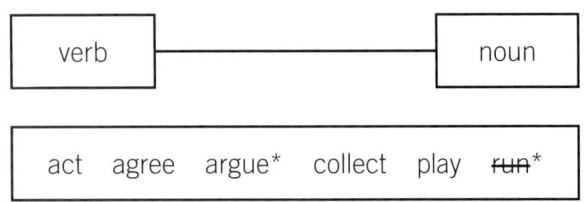

verb → noun

act   agree   argue*   collect   play   ~~run~~*

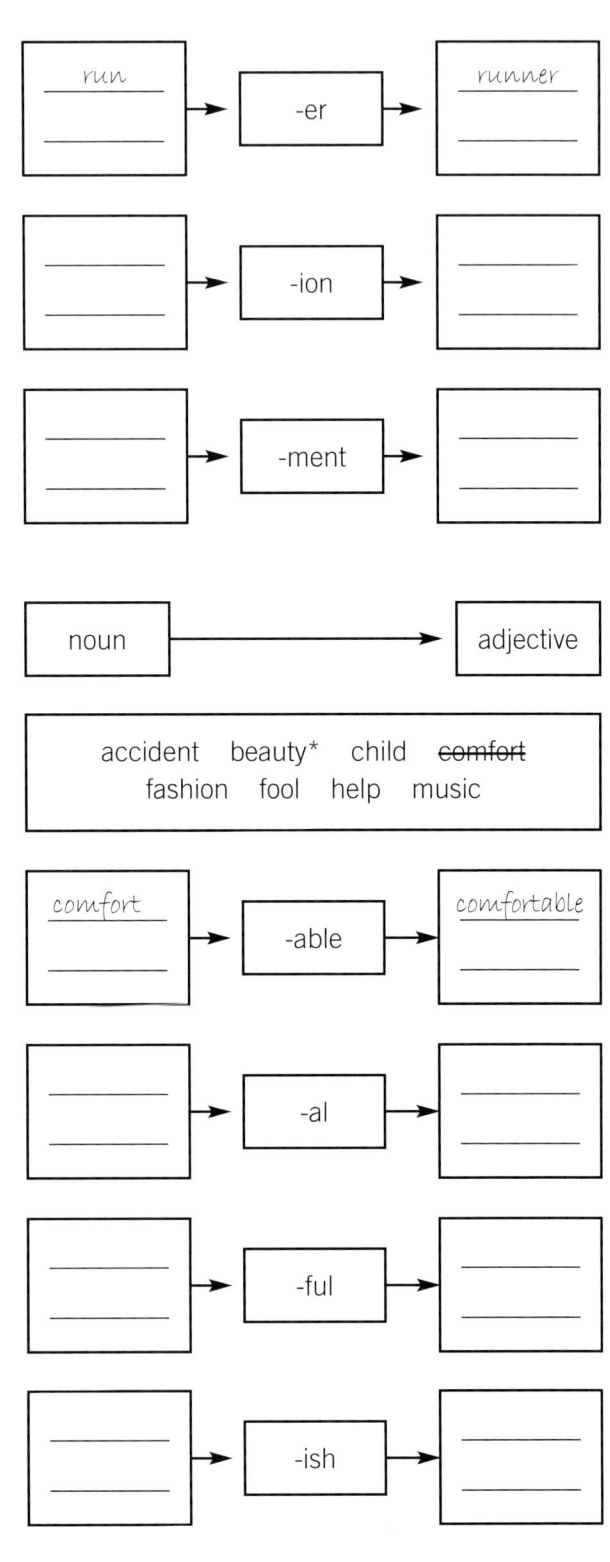

run → -er → runner

___ → -ion → ___

___ → -ment → ___

noun → adjective

accident   beauty*   child   ~~comfort~~
fashion   fool   help   music

comfort → -able → comfortable

___ → -al → ___

___ → -ful → ___

___ → -ish → ___

Personal Identity — UNIT 7

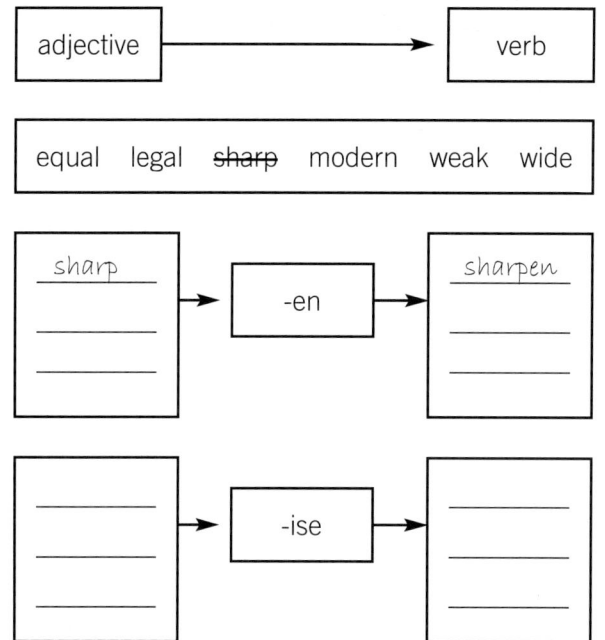

equal legal ~~sharp~~ modern weak wide

3 Suffixes

Core grammar

Now write one of the words below in each of the spaces. Use your dictionary if you need it.

> agreement argument childish
> collection loosen modernise musical
> sharpen weaken widen

1 It's likely the pound will _____ against the dollar in the next month or so.
2 If the union and management don't reach an _____ the strike will go ahead.
3 Phil can play five different _____ instruments.
4 Every time Lucia and Gavin are in a meeting they have an _____.
5 Georgio has a nice _____ of old jazz records.
6 This road's too narrow – they should _____ it.
7 I can't _____ these screws. I'll need a bigger screwdriver.
8 You should _____ this knife – it can't cut these tomatoes.
9 Your behaviour is very _____. Try to grow up a bit.
10 They took out a bank loan because they wanted to _____ their house.

4 Comparatives

Core grammar

Use each group of words below and write a sentence. Make a comparison. The first one is done for you.

Glasgow, Dundee, bigger _Glasgow is bigger than Dundee._

1 Tigers, tortoises, faster _____
2 Curry, salad, hot _____
3 Aberdeen, Paris, cold _____
4 Cars, bicycles, expensive _____
5 Motorways, country roads, wide _____
6 Skiing, table-tennis, dangerous _____
7 People, cats, intelligent _____
8 Horror films, comedies, frightening _____

5 Present simple and continuous

Core grammar

Look at these sentences. Some of them use verbs that don't work in the present continuous. Put a tick (✔) after the correct ones and a cross (✘) after the wrong ones.

1 The dog's running around the garden. _____
2 These shoes aren't fitting. Do you have a larger pair? _____
3 Marcia's having a new coat. _____
4 The satellite connection isn't working again. _____
5 Don't worry about it – it isn't mattering. _____
6 Susan's working in the library today. _____
7 I'm not knowing much about science. _____
8 I'm really thinking this isn't a good idea. _____
9 I'm thinking about my family. _____
10 I'm not wanting any more coffee. _____

UNIT 7 Personal Identity

6 Present simple and continuous
Core grammar
Some of the verbs below don't work in the present continuous. Write each one either in the **present simple** or the **present continuous**.

1 'What …….. you …….. (**do**)?' 'I work with computers.'
2 'Go away – I …….. (**have**) a bath!'
3 I …….. (**not feel**) this is right.
4 'Hi – I …….. (**phone**) from the bus. I'll see you soon.
5 He …….. (**score**) a lot of goals this season.
6 '…….. you …….. (**see**) the cat? It's up that tree.'
7 'Something …….. (**smell**) good – what are you cooking?
8 I like my car – I …….. (not **want**) a new one.
9 Don't order fish for Jane – she …….. (**hate**) it.
10 The plane …….. (**land**) right now – we'll see him in a few minutes.

7 Family members, step- and half-
Vocabulary
Look at Lorraine's family tree. Write one relationship from the box for each question **1-10** on page 29.

> half-brother half-sister stepbrother
> stepdaughter stepdaughters stepfather
> stepfather stepmother stepsister stepson

| John and Louise had three children, Andy, Lorraine and Carol, then they got divorced. |

| John later married Claire, and they had a son, Luke. |

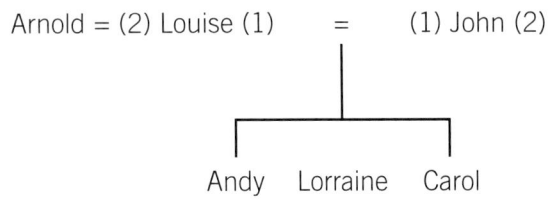

Arnold = (2) Louise (1)   =   (1) John (2)   =   (2) Claire (1)   =   Matthew

Andy Lorraine Carol   Luke   Emily   Joshua

| Then Louise married Arnold. |

| Before this, Claire was married to Matthew and they had two children, Emily and Joshua. Then Mathew died in a car crash. |

8 Comparative and superlative adverbs
Grammar extension
Change each adverb in bold to its comparative or superlative form.

1 If he learns to run a bit (**fast**) he'll get into the team.
2 What kind of music do you like (**well**)?
3 Sandra's working (**hard**) than she did last year.
4 The flooding affected this street (**bad**) of all parts of the town.
5 She speaks Polish (**fluent**) than English.
6 My computer's working (**well**) now than before.
7 You need to think about this (**careful**) than you usually do.
8 Of the students in the class, Marta travels from (**far**) away but she usually arrives (**early**).
9 Try to speak to her (**sensitive**) than you usually do.

28

1 Luke is Lorraine's _____.
2 Emily is Lorraine's _____.
3 Joshua is Lorraine's _____.
4 Arnold is Lorraine's _____.
5 Claire is Lorraine's _____.
6 Carol is Luke's _____.
7 Andy is Arnold's _____.
8 Lorraine and Carol are Arnold's _____.
9 Emily is John's _____.
10 John is Joshua's _____.

9 Writing

Think about people you know – married couples, boyfriends and girlfriends or just pairs of friends. Why do you think they like each other? In what ways are they similar or different? Describe a couple you know and why you think they stay together.

_____
_____
_____
_____
_____
_____
_____
_____
_____

10 Pronunciation

Look at the example below. A **heel** is part of a shoe. It sounds the same as **he'll**. Write the other words on the lines.

he'll   part of a shoe _heel_

1 great   break food down into small pieces _____
2 plane   clear and simple _____
3 rays   lift up _____
4 stake   piece of meat _____
5 sail   selling something _____
6 steal   metal _____
7 stationery   not moving _____
8 tail   story _____
9 weighed   walk through water _____
10 wait   how heavy something is _____
11 leak   vegetable _____
12 cent   perfume _____

UNIT 8
Daily Life

1 Past simple: *yes/no* questions and short answers

Core grammar

Work with a partner. Change the order of the words to make questions and short answers.

Example:

job it it a yes was good was

Was _____ _____ _____ _____? _____, _____ _____.

Was   it   a   good   job?   Yes,   it   was.

1 you did yes the enjoy film did I

   Did _____ _____ _____ _____ _____?

   _____, _____ _____.

2 she yes out was last was she night

   _____ _____ _____ _____ _____ was.?

   _____, _____ _____.

3 didn't no apply did job she for the Anna

   _____ _____ _____ _____ _____ _____

   _____? _____, _____ didn't.

4 did Fraser China did he last go to year yes

   _____ _____ _____ _____ _____ _____

   _____ _____? _____, _____ _____.

5 party wasn't at were I the you no

   _____ _____ _____ _____ _____ _____?

   _____, _____ _____.

6 at no same weren't were they the they school

   _____ _____ _____ _____ _____ _____

   _____? _____, _____ _____.

2 Past simple: *wh-* questions

Core grammar

Read this:

Last night Baz and Imran went to the cinema. They paid seven pounds for two seats. The film was quite violent and Imran didn't like it. After the film they missed the bus. They walked back to Baz's flat and arrived at half-past eleven. After that, they drank coffee.

Now use the words below to make questions in the past simple, and answer them.

Who/Baz go out with? 'Who did Baz go out with?'
'Imran.'

1 Where/go? '_____,'
   '_____,'

2 How much/cost?
   '_____,'
   '_____,'

3 Why/not like the film?
   '_____,'
   '_____,'

4 Why/walk back to Baz's flat?
   '_____,'
   '_____,'

5 When/arrive? '_____,'
   '_____,'

6 What/do after that?
   '_____,'
   '_____,'

Daily Life UNIT 8

3 Past simple: negatives

Core grammar

Change the sentences below to their negative form.
The first one is done for you.

I went out last night. '*I didn't go out last night.*' I stayed in.'
1 I finished the coffee. '_____.' Amy did.'
2 I switched off the TV. '_____.' It's still on.'
3 Marta went to Rome. '_____.' She went to Paris.'
4 I drove to London. '_____.' I flew.'
5 I had a holiday last year. '_____.' I stayed at home.'
6 Nasreen lied to me. '_____.' She told the truth.'
7 They went for a drink. '_____.' They went to the cinema.'
8 We met in New York. '_____.' We met in Boston.'

4 Past simple: irregular verbs

Core grammar

Decide which group, **1–6**, each verb in the box belongs to. Write all three parts on the lines.

become	buy	choose	come	cost	drink
fly	freeze	grow	hear	know	let	mean
put	shake	sing	swim	teach

Group 1

All three parts are the same.

base form	past simple	past participle
1 =	2 =	3
_____	_____	_____
_____	_____	_____
_____	_____	_____

Group 2

Parts 1 and 3 are the same. Part 2 is different.

base form	past simple	past participle
1	=	3
_____	_____	_____
_____	_____	_____

Group 3

Parts 1 and 2 are different. Part 2 is the same as Part 3.

base form	past simple	past participle
1 ≠	2 =	3
_____	_____	_____
_____	_____	_____
_____	_____	_____
_____	_____	_____
_____	_____	_____

Group 4

All three parts are different. Part 3 ends with *–en*.

base form	past simple	past participle
1 ≠	2 ≠	3 = -en
_____	_____	_____
_____	_____	_____
_____	_____	_____

Group 5

All three parts are different. Part 2 ends with *–ew*. Part 3 ends with *–n*.

base form	past simple	past participle
1 ≠	2 = -ew ≠	3 = -n
_____	_____	_____
_____	_____	_____
_____	_____	_____

UNIT 8 Daily Life

Group 6

All three parts are different. Part 1 has *i*, Part 2 has *a* and Part 3 has *u*.

base form		past simple		past participle
1 = i	≠	2 = a	≠	3 = u
_____		_____		_____
_____		_____		_____
_____		_____		_____

5 *lie* and *lay*

Grammar extension

For each sentence **1–5** decide whether **a**, **b** or **both** are correct. Tick (✔) the boxes.

1. He lied all morning
   a. He didn't tell the truth all morning. ☐
   b. He stayed in bed till lunchtime. ☐

2. She's not lying.
   a. She's telling the truth. ☐
   b. She's sitting, kneeling or standing. ☐

3. Josh lain the books on the shelf.
   a. Josh put the books on the shelf. ☐
   b. *This sentence is bad English.* ☐

4. The soldiers laid down their arms.
   a. The soldiers relaxed. ☐
   b. The soldiers gave up their weapons. ☐

6 Positions

Vocabulary

Write two of the jobs or positions in the box after each of the areas of work below.

> anaesthetist   backbencher   bishop
> branch secretary   captain   commis chef
> constable   councillor   director   elder
> headteacher   inspector   kitchen porter
> lecturer   midwife   principal teacher
> private   professor   provost
> secretary of state   shareholder   shop steward

politics   _____ _____

restaurant   _____ _____

school   _____ _____

local government _____ _____

army   _____ _____

church   _____ _____

company   _____ _____

police   _____ _____

hospital   _____ _____

university   _____ _____

trade union   _____ _____

7 Writing

Think of life 100 years ago. What were the main differences from life today? What things today did people not have then? How was life different in those days? Do you think it was better of worse? Were people happier or less happy? Write your ideas here.

Daily Life — UNIT 8

8 Pronunciation

Decide if each verb below ends in /t/, /d/ or /ɪd/.
Put a tick (✔) on one line after each verb.

	/t/	/d/	/ɪd/
hated			
decided			
rushed			
hoped			
ended			
saved			
closed			
picked			
grabbed			
landed			
coughed			
touched			
dodged			
wasted			
missed			

UNIT 9
Physical Environment

1 *can* for permission

Core grammar

Read the information below. Each time, make a request using **can**. Use the words given.

No parking
Mon-Fri, 9.00-5.30
Except bank holidays and Wednesdays in August

1 _____ _____ park here?

2 _____ _____ _____ this ticket now?

Only senior students and their guests are allowed in this Common Room

3 _____ _____ _____ in?

No dogs allowed in shop except guide dogs *and small cute cuddly dogs!*

4 _____ _____ _____ my dog in?

Absolutely nobody is allowed to walk on this grass.

Exceptions:
lecturers at weekends.
parents and their children on Parents' Day.

5 _____ _____ _____ on _____ _____ ?

6 _____ _____ _____ pie, chips and peas?

2 can for ability, may for probability

Core grammar

Choose between **can/can't** or **may/may not** in each sentence.

1 Of course I **can/may** swim – I just don't want to today.
2 Check the calendar – it **can/may** be her birthday today.
3 I'm not sure – she **can't/may not** be at home at this time of day – but give her a ring anyway.
4 Bill **can't/may not** tell jokes – somebody should tell him he isn't funny.
5 '**Can/may** you really play the bagpipes?' 'Yes, I learned at school.'
6 OK, he **can't/may not** win but he's but he's a good horse and I'm going to put ten pounds on him.
7 I **can't/may not** get to the party but I'll try.
8 'We **can/may** afford that house but I'm not sure I like it.'

3 can, can't, could, couldn't

Grammar extension

Look at the sentences below. In each one, write **can**, **can't**, **could** or **couldn't** on the line.

1 My sister _____ cut hair. Do you want her to do yours?
2 Look, shut up, will you? You know you _____ sing.
3 I _____ go out tonight but I really should finish this essay. I'll stay in.
4 She just went to Majorca and found a job. I _____ do that.
5 I wonder if you _____ possibly … perhaps … lend me fifty quid?
6 Where _____ I buy a newspaper around here?
7 I'm sorry, I _____ help you. I don't know anything about it.
8 You _____ park here before six. Go somewhere else.
9 She _____ live in London but she prefers the country.
10 Quite honestly I _____ care less.

4 could or might

Grammar extension

Choose the best form in each sentence below.

1 **Could/might** you get me a cup of coffee?
2 '**Couldn't/mightn't** you ask for a day off work on Friday?' 'OK, I'll speak to the _____ boss.'
3 She's the best candidate but she **couldn't/mightn't** get the job. We'll have to wait and see.
4 I **couldn't/mightn't** care less what he thinks.
5 I don't have time to cook tonight – **could/might** you order a takeaway?
6 I **could/might** tell Marge what I think but I won't.
7 'Cheer up – it **couldn't/might not** happen.' 'Oh yes, it will.'
8 Pass me that magazine – I **could/might** read it on the train.

5 might

Grammar extension

What do you think that people would say when looking at these pictures? Write your ideas on the lines. The first one is done for you.

He might score.

UNIT 9 Physical Environment

1 _____

3 _____

2 _____

4 _____

6 Vocabulary

Look this picture of a town centre. Write one word from the box on each line

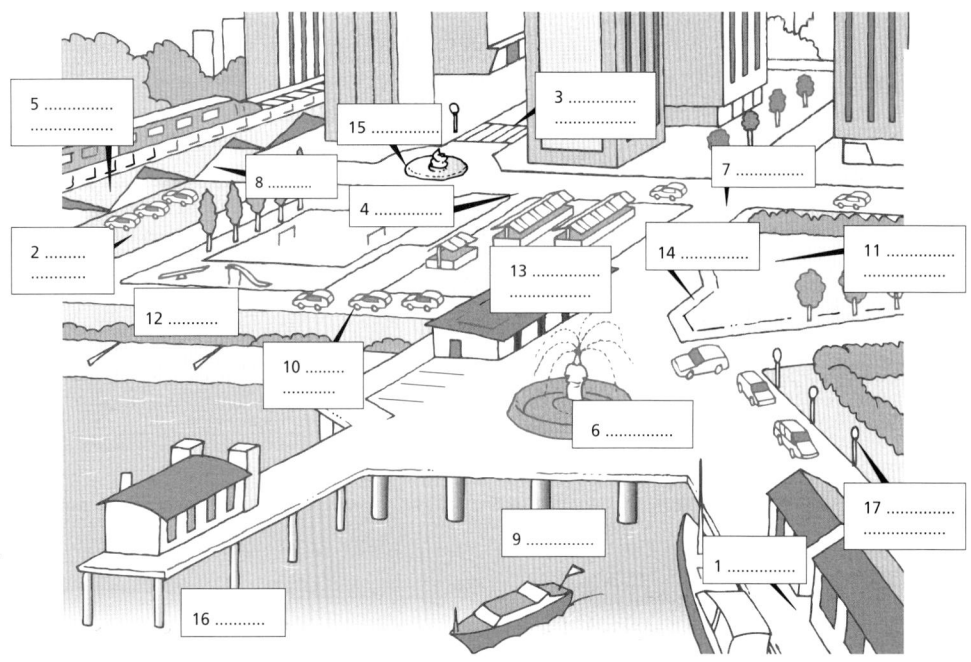

alley   car park   crossroads   fountain   harbour   junction   park   parking meters
pavement   pedestrian precinct   pier   railway bridge   roundabout   street market
subway   taxi rank   zebra crossing

7 Weather

Vocabulary

Here are some weather symbols from the BBC Weather Centre. Write one name from the box under each symbol.

> black, low level cloud   hail
> light rain shower   heavy rain
> thundery shower   light snow
> heavy snow   sleet   sunny
> sunny intervals

_____

_____

_____

_____

_____

_____

_____

_____

_____

_____

8 Writing

You win ten million pounds on the State Lottery. You decide to buy a house for yourself – and maybe your family. What kind of house would you like to buy? Where would you like your house to be – in any part of the world?

UNIT 9 Physical Environment

Write about your dream house and your favourite location.

9 Pronunciation

The unfinished words below are all in course book Unit 9. They have four different stress patterns. Write one letter on each line to finish them.

●••

aerop __ __ __ __

moto __ __ __ __ __

passe __ __ __ __

•●•

demol __ __ __

locat __ __ __

recyc __ __ __ __

•●••

abil __ __ __

faciliti __ __

histor __ __ __ __

••●•

econo __ __ __ __

entertainm __ __ __

conserv __ __ __ __ __

UNIT 10
Social Environment

1 Present perfect: past participles
Core grammar
All the past participles below are wrong. Correct them.

1 Maria has sang that song before.
2 The kids have broke another window.
3 Oops! I've throwed the ball into the neighbour's garden.
4 They've drank all the coffee.
5 Has Shabnam woke up yet?
6 Who has drew that cartoon on the blackboard?
7 It's winter but the sun has shined all day.
8 Have you flied many times before?

2 Present perfect: statements
Core grammar
Write the verbs in (**bold**) in their present perfect form.

1 Sandra (**finish**) _____ her lunch.
2 Muhammad and Rushna (**come**) _____ to see you.
3 Mike (**visit**) _____ Paris.
4 Oh no! I (**break**) _____ another cup.
5 She (**eat**) _____ the last cake.
6 We (**see**) _____ that film before.
7 My parents (**send**) _____ me some money.
8 The rain (**start**) _____ again.

3 Present perfect: questions and negatives
Core grammar
Make these sentences into questions or negatives. Follow the signs: **?** or **−**

1 − He's left the country. _____
2 ? Mikel's gone to play tennis. _____
3 ? Who you have spoken to. _____
4 − I've finished my essay. _____
5 − This has happened before. _____
6 ? How long you have lived here. _____
7 − Irina's had lunch. _____
7 ? You've seen that film before. _____
9 ? Why he has left. _____
10 − I've met your sister. _____
11 ? The cat has gone out. _____
12 ? Where he has gone. _____

4 Present perfect with *been* or *gone*
Core grammar
Complete the answers to these questions using **been** or **gone**.

1 'Where are Tomas and Marcia?' 'They've _____ to the football match.'
2 'Hi – you look different.' 'Well, I've _____ to the hairdresser's.'
3 'That restaurant's awful.' 'How do you know? Have you _____ there?'
4 'Is Anne at home?' 'No, sorry, She's _____ to the shops.'
5 'Do you know anything about Latvia?' 'Well, actually, I've _____ there a couple of times.'

UNIT 10 Social Environment

6 'Where has Petra _____?' 'Oh, she's off home. She left ten minutes ago.'

7 Of course I can add up the bill – I've _____ to school.

8 Thanks for your email. Rick has _____ to Bucharest and will deal with it when he gets back on Friday.

5 Present perfect or past simple

Core grammar

Write the verbs below in the **present perfect** or the **past simple**.

1 Mike (**take**) _____ Cheryl to see a film last night.

2 I (**see**) _____ Alan just before 10 o'clock.

3 Look! Jack (**buy**) _____ a new car.

4 Rohan isn't here now. He (**go**) _____ home.

5 She (**buy**) _____ that dress last year.

6 Julia just (**drop**) _____ your phone on the floor.

7 The train (**arrive**) _____ five minutes ago.

8 Oh no! I (**leave**) _____ my diary at home.

9 I (**tell**) _____ him the whole story last week.

6 Present perfect or past simple

Core grammar

In each pair, choose which sentence, **a** or **b**, is correct.

1 a When did you arrive here?
   b When have you arrived here?

2 a When has he left?
   b When did he leave?

3 a When did you last see Sandila?
   b When have you last seen Sandila?

4 a How many times have you read that book?
   b How many times do you read that book?

5 a When has Lorna gone to Sheffield?
   b When did Lorna go to Sheffield?

7 Present perfect or past simple

Core grammar

Each of these sentences uses the present perfect or the past simple. Some are correct and others are wrong. Tick (✔) the correct ones and correct the wrong ones.

1 She's lived in Italy before she came here. ___

2 I think I met him some time before. ___

3 Sunee's birthday was last week. ___

4 Darren's flown back to Ireland for the weekend. ___

5 When I was your age I have spent a lot of money on clothes. ___

6 Who has lived in that flat last year? ___

7 She's around here somewhere – I've seen her five minutes ago. ___

8 I've forgotten to buy bread again. ___

9 Where have you gone last night? ___

10 Sonia left about an hour ago. ___

8 Present perfect or past simple

Core grammar

Read the sentences and answer the questions. Tick (✔) the correct answer.

1 He had a long and interesting life.
   Is he alive now? **yes/no**

2 My car has broken down. *Is it OK now?* **yes/no**

3 Ricky has bought a new t-shirt.
   Does he have a new t-shirt now? **yes/no**

4 Keira once went to Paris for a holiday.
   Is she still in Paris? **yes/no**

5 Colin's father has gone to hospital.
   Is he there now? **yes/no**

6 My brother has shaved off his beard.
   Does he have a beard now? **yes/no**

7 We bought a new house yesterday.
   Do we still own it? **yes/no**

Social Environment UNIT 10

9 Present perfect or past simple

Core grammar

Choose the better ending for each sentence below.

1 I cooked the lunch
   a so you cook the dinner.
   b so come and eat.

2 Mario's opened a new restaurant
   a so let's go and eat there.
   b but it didn't make any money.

3 I've met Maria's Canadian friend
   a last week.
   b and I don't like him.

4 Vera bought a car
   a – it's really nice.
   b from that dealer.

5 We've won the game
   a – that's brilliant!
   b the last time we played them.

6 I've been to that shop a few times
   a before it closed.
   b recently.

7 Terry hasn't had a haircut
   a this term.
   b last week.

8 Did you see that film
   a yet?
   b when it was in the cinemas?

10 Present perfect or past simple

Core grammar

Decide which sentence, **a** or **b**, better follows each question **1–8**.

1 'Hi. Why are you looking so healthy?'
   a 'I've been on holiday.'
   b 'I went on holiday.'

2 'What do you know about French food?'
   a 'Well, I've lived to France.'
   b 'Well, I lived in France.'

3 'How was your weekend?'
   a 'Very nice. We've been skiing.'
   b 'Very nice. We went skiing.'

4 'Do you know Liverpool at all?'
   a 'Yes, I've been there a couple of times.'
   b 'Yes, I went there a couple of times.'

5 'And what happened after that?'
   a 'Well, Tim has turned and walked away.'
   b 'Well, Tim turned and walked away.'

6 'What's the panic?'
   a 'Luigi's cut himself. Get a bandage!'
   b 'Luigi cut himself. Get a bandage!'

7 'Do you know anything about Italy?'
   a 'A bit. I've had a holiday there last year.'
   b 'A bit. I had a holiday there last year.'

8 'What's wrong with the photocopier?'
   a 'Oh, it's broken down yesterday.'
   b 'Oh, it broke down yesterday.'

41

UNIT 10 Social Environment

11 Present perfect or past simple

Core grammar

Read this e-mail from Nick Hanrahan, an Australian now living in London, to a friend back home in Tasmania. Decide whether each verb should be in the **present perfect** or the **past simple**.

To:
Subject:

G'day mate,

Well, (1) **I've been/I was** in London now for three weeks so (2) **I've thought/I thought** I'd drop you a line. (3) **I've been/I was** totally exhausted when (4) **I've got/I got** here after the long flight, and, I tell you, (5) **it's been/it was** all a bit of a shock for the first few days ... weeks maybe. (6) **It has rained/It rained** the day (7) **I arrived/I've arrived** and I think (8) **it rained/it's rained** every day since. No, I'm exaggerating a bit mate, but it's a lot colder and wetter than Oz. I suppose you have to expect that, but in the first couple of weeks (9) **I've had/I had** to try hard to get used to it.

London's like – very big. Just remember, before I came here, the biggest place (10) **I've known/I knew** was Hobart. It isn't just the size, though, it's the different types of people. (11) **I've never seen/I never saw** so many races and cultures and languages in one place. I suppose Sydney is a bit like that, but (12) **I've never been/I never went** to Sydney, apart from changing planes at the airport. The best thing, though, is the food. Back in Tassie, people told me that pommy food was bad, but they didn't tell me about all the different types you can buy, either in restaurants or supermarkets. (13) **I've eaten/I ate** Indian, Chinese, Thai, Mexican, Italian, Spanish – you name it, (14) **I've eaten it/I ate it**. OK, you can get all that stuff in Oz in the cities, but not in our local shop.

Right, mate, have to close now. Get back to me.

Cheers,

Nick

Now find the Australian words Nick uses for these:

Hello _____   Australia _____

British _____   Tasmania _____

12 Present perfect and past simple with *for*, *since*, *yet* and *ago*.

Grammar extension

Write *for*, *since*, *yet* or *ago* in the correct place in each of the sentences below.

1 Laura isn't here. She went home ten minutes _____.

2 Don't touch the chocolate – I haven't paid for it _____.

3 They've lived in that house _____ about twenty years.

4 It's a new shop – it only opened a couple of weeks _____.

5 _____ you were here last a lot of things have changed.

6 Hi Kaeko – I haven't seen you _____ ages.

7 I can't come out. I haven't finished my homework _____.

8 I've waited _____ days for this letter to arrive.

9 I've known about this _____ last week.

Social Environment — UNIT 10

10 'I've been to Paris.' 'How long _____ was that?'

11 Jeremy's been off work _____ Tuesday.

12 'Who did it?' 'I haven't found out _____.'

13 used to / (be) used to

Core grammar

Write the correct form of **used to** or **(be) used to** on the lines below.

1 Khalil and Sadia _____ live in a flat but they bought a bungalow last year.

2 I've been here in Nigeria for two years and I _____ the heat now.

3 Jason _____ working on the nightshift now.

4 He _____ play computer games for hours when he was younger.

5 Jim _____ getting up quite early.

6 Freda can be quite grumpy sometimes but I _____ it.

7 I _____ cycle to work but the days are too short now.

8 I don't need help – I _____ doing things on my own.

9 See that guy? He _____ be a millionaire but he went bankrupt.

14 Relationships

Vocabulary

Read the sentences that follow. These show different things that happen in a relationship. Match one of the letters **a–k** to each number **1–10** on the lines below.

1 _____   7 _____
2 _____   8 _____
3 _____   9 _____
4 _____   10 _____
5 _____
6 _____

a Jack fancies Jill. Jill fancies Jack.

b They get engaged.

c They start to go steady.

d Jack chats Jill up. /Jill chats Jack up.

e They get married.

f Jack meets Jill's family. Jill meets Jack's family.

g They get divorced.

h They break up./They separate.

i After a while, they don't get on very well.

j They go out together.

15 Writing

There are many charities in Britain. They collect money in the streets, they have television appeals and they run charity shops. They collect money for children, for people with illnesses, for animals and for emergencies like earthquakes. People give money to charities but some think that they shouldn't be necessary because governments should do more. What do you think? Write your ideas here:

_____
_____
_____
_____
_____
_____
_____
_____
_____
_____
_____
_____
_____
_____

UNIT 10 Social Environment

16 Pronunciation

Look at the underlined letters in the words below. Think of their consonant sounds. Write one word on each line.

> ankle   beige   chair   thing   jam   machine
> nature   shop   singer   teeth   they   this
> urgent   usual

θ _____   _____

ð _____   _____

ʃ _____   _____

ʒ _____   _____

tʃ _____   _____

dʒ _____   _____

ŋ _____   _____

UNIT 11
Free Time

1 must and have to: questions and negatives

Core grammar

Make these sentences into questions and negatives. Remember to use question marks when necessary.

1 ? 'You must play your music so loud.'
   _____

2 – 'You have to leave so early.'
   _____

3 ? 'She have to come with us.'
   _____

4 ? 'Why you have to do that.'
   _____

5 ? 'They must lose so many games.'
   _____

6 ? 'You really have to go to work today.'
   _____

7 – 'She must see him again.'
   _____

8 ? 'What I must do to be in the team.'
   _____

9 – 'You must talk in here.'
   _____

10 ? 'Where I have to go now?'
   _____

11 – 'I have to work.'
   _____

12 ? 'When I have to finish this.'
   _____

2 must and have to

Core grammar

Write **must** or **have to/has to** on each line below.

1 I _____ sell my car. I can't afford it any more.

2 I'm really overweight. I _____ go on a diet.

3 Joe's leaving now – he _____ home by nine.

4 Before you get this job we _____ see your college certificates.

5 You _____ get out and walk more – it's very good for you.

6 You don't _____ be mad to work in this office – but it helps.

7 You _____ wash your hair more often. It looks horrible.

8 Natalia _____ work harder at school – her marks are terrible.

9 You _____ drive on the left in Britain. All the other drivers do.

3 must and should

Core grammar

Choose between **must** and **should** in the sentences below.

1 I can't come out tonight. I've got an essay and I **must/should** finish it for tomorrow or the teacher will be very angry.

2 'My eyes hurt when I go out in bright sunlight.'
   'Well, you **must/should** wear sunglasses.'
   'I know, but I don't like them.'

3 Look at all the litter in the streets. The police **must/should** do something about it – but they probably won't.

4 'We lost 3–0. That's five matches without a win.'
   'Yes, we **must/should** win some games soon or we'll be out of the league next year.'

45

UNIT 11 Free Time

5 'I think Emma's lovely but she never speaks to me.'
'Well, maybe you **must/should** speak to her.'
'I know – the thing is, I can't think of what to say.'

4 *must*, *have to* and *should*

Choose the best form in each sentence:

1

Do you want to go out on the bikes today?

OK, but I've got a flat tyre. I **have to/should** fix it first.

2

BASIC HILLWALKING

Jeans are not good in cold weather. Heavy trousers are better. Many different types are

Walkers **have to/should** wear heavy trousers in cold weather.

3

I'm sorry, you **have to/should** make an appointment before you see a doctor. Now, Dr McKay's free at three o'clock tomorrow.

4

Tell him I **must/should** have an answer today. Tomorrow's no good.

Nice seeing you. We **have to/must** meet for lunch some day.

5 *must* for obligation and deduction

Grammar extension

Read the sentences below. Each ending, **a** or **b**, is more likely to suggest either **obligation** or **deduction** as a meaning for **must**. Tick one box in each column for each sentence 1–6.

obligation   deduction

I must get up early tomorrow – I've got some work to finish.

You must be joking. You never get up before lunchtime on Sundays.

	obligation	deduction
1 She must see her doctor		
a before things get worse.	☐	☐
b every week – she always thinks she's ill.	☐	☐
2 They must live here		
a – it's a beautiful house and I'm sure they'll be happy in it.	☐	☐
b – I checked the address.	☐	☐
3 He must get up at seven		
a – he goes for a swim before work.	☐	☐
b if he wants to catch the plane.	☐	☐
4 You must know the safety rules		
a – you can't do this job if you don't.	☐	☐
b – I told you them last week.	☐	☐
5 You must eat a lot		
a – you're overweight.	☐	☐
b – you're underweight.	☐	☐
6 Nerma must study hard		
a – she always looks tired.	☐	☐
b to get a good degree.	☐	☐

Free Time UNIT 11

6 Musical instruments

Vocabulary

Write the name of each musical instrument under its picture.

> bagpipes   banjo   cello   clarinet   drums
> flute   guitar   harmonica/mouth organ   harp
> piano   trumpet

1 _____

2 _____

3 _____

4 _____

5 _____

6 _____

7 _____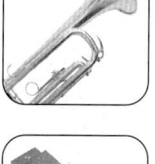

8 _____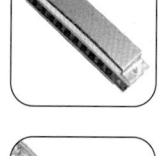

9 _____

10 _____

7 Music

Vocabulary

Match each word numbered 1–12 with its meaning in the list a–l.

1 album
2 ballad
3 brass band
4 classical music
5 duet
6 hymn
7 gig
8 opera
9 orchestra
10 pipe band
11 soundtrack
12 group

a a song that is sung by two people
b the music from a film
c a band where the musicians play bagpipes and drums
d a band in which the musicians play metal instruments like trumpet and trombone
e a large group of musicians who usually play classical music
f a CD with a number of songs or pieces of music on it
g a musical play where the performers sing most of the words
h a small number of performers who sing and play instruments together
i a live performance by a singer or group
j a song that tells a story
k serious music that has been popular for a long time
l a serious song that is usually sung in church

47

UNIT 11 Free Time

8 Writing

A friend from another country is coming to stay with you for a week. He/she sends you this email –

Think of a few places in your area, or further away, that you and your friend can visit over a week. Answer the email and describe them.

9 Pronunciation

Send

To:
Subject:

Hi,

I'm really looking forward to coming to see you. But, tell me, what is there to do in your town? I've checked the internet and seen some of the things but you live there. You know I like all kinds of places – art galleries, museums, historical stuff, the countryside … Could you maybe suggest a few places to visit and I can read up on them on the internet?

In each group of four words, one has a different vowel sound. <u>Underline</u> it. The first one has been done for you.

	laid	paid	raid	<u>said</u>
1	bone	cone	gone	phone
2	does	goes	hoes	toes
3	con	son	ton	won
4	catch	hatch	match	watch
5	charm	farm	harm	warm
6	cart	dart	part	wart
7	bull	dull	full	pull
8	could	mould	should	would
9	lint	mint	pint	tint

UNIT 12
Finding Work

1 mustn't or needn't/not have to
Core grammar
Write **mustn't** or **don't/doesn't have to** on each line below. (Remember that **needn't** means the same as **not have to**. If you prefer, you can write it instead.)

1 You _____ cut the grass. I did it before you woke up.

2 Louisa's pregnant – she _____ drink alcohol.

3 Britta _____ stay out in the sun so long – it's very bad for her skin.

4 He _____ arrive exactly on time. It doesn't matter if he's a few minutes late.

5 You _____ let Carl cook – he's useless in the kitchen.

6 You _____ pick me up at the airport – I can get a taxi into town.

7 Tell Ayesha she _____ come to the meeting if she's too busy.

8 Ben – put that piece of wood down. You _____ hit your little brother.

2 Past simple or past continuous
Core grammar
Decide if each verb below should be in the past simple or past continuous. Both verbs might be in the past simple, or both in the past continuous, or there might be one of each.

1 The letter (**arrive**) _____ while I (**have**) _____ breakfast.

2 Bert (**drive**) _____ on the wrong side of the road when he (**have**) _____ _____ the accident.

3 When the film (**end**) _____ Lorraine got up and (**make**) _____ some coffee.

4 Hassan (**lie**) _____ in the bath when the lights (**go**) _____ out.

5 The fire bell still (**ring**) _____ when the firemen (**get**) _____ there.

6 I (**live**) _____ in Australia when they (**get**) _____ married.

7 He (**become**) _____ famous when he (**win**) _____ the Grand National.

8 Who (**take**) _____ this photo when you (**sit**) _____ on the beach?

UNIT 12 Finding Work

3 Past perfect

Core grammar

Rewrite the past simple forms on the left as past perfect forms.

	past simple	past perfect
	it began	it had begun
1	it broke	
2	I built	
3	we bought	
4	he caught	
5	she chose	
6	they cost	
7	you drank	
8	she drove	
9	I ate	
10	you fell	
11	I flew	
12	she forgot	
13	I gave	
14	he grew	
15	I heard	
16	it hurt	
17	we met	
18	I rang	
19	it shone	
20	they slept	
21	I stood	
22	we swam	
23	she taught	
24	I thought	

4 Past simple or past perfect

Core grammar

This is Jake. He's the manager of one of the most successful restaurants in town and he's talking about how he got this job. Decide if the verbs in brackets should be in the past simple or the past perfect. Write the correct form on the line.

It was a Monday afternoon and I **1 (be)** _____ out of a job for three weeks and the money **2 (begin)** _____ to run low. Also, I **3 (start)** _____ some bad habits, like going to bed late and getting up at lunchtime. Anyway, I went to the Job Centre but there **4 (be)** _____ nothing interesting there. So then I **5 (decide)** _____ to take a walk and when I **6 (wander)** _____ round for an hour or so I **7 (see)** _____ an advert in a restaurant window. It **8 (say)** _____ 'Kitchen Porter required.' Well, you know what kitchen porter means – it means dishwasher most of the time – but it **9 (look)** _____ like a nice place so I **10 (go)** _____ in and **11 (ask)** _____.

The manager **12 (say)** _____ they **13 (be)** _____ open for just three weeks and I **14 (like)** _____ the idea of being part of a new restaurant. I **15 (work)** _____ as a kitchen porter when I was living in Paris so I **16 (knew)** _____ something about it. Anyway, two days later the chef **17 (be)** _____ ill and the manager **18 (ask)** _____ me if I could cook. I said yes because I **19 (do)** _____ some cooking. Anyway, he **20 (like)** _____ what I **21 (cook)** _____ and the chef never **22 (come)** _____ back – in fact he **23 (leave)** _____ town three weeks later.

So I **24 (stay)** _____ on as chef and then I **25 (get)** _____ to be assistant manager. How? Well, by that time I **26 (meet)** _____ Simona and a few months later we got married. Oh, I **27 (forget)** _____ to mention this – she's the manager's daughter. So he **28 (think)** _____ I **29 (be)** _____ OK as assistant manager and he **30 (decide)** _____ to retire and now I'm the manager. So my advice is, if you don't know what to do, go for a walk.

Finding Work UNIT 12

5 Past continuous or past perfect
Core grammar
Decide whether sentence **B** or sentence **C** is closer to the meaning of sentence **A**. Tick (✔) one of the boxes.

1. **A** I left before he made the speech.
   B I had left when he made the speech. ☐
   C I left when he had made the speech. ☐

2. **A** He ran the last few metres and just caught the train.
   B The train was leaving when he got to the station. ☐
   C The train had left when he got to the station. ☐

3. **A** He fell off his bike because he was laughing.
   B He laughed when he fell off his bike. ☐
   C He was laughing when he fell off his bike. ☐

4. **A** We missed the first ten minutes of the game.
   B The game was starting when we got there. ☐
   C The game had started when we got there. ☐

5. **A** He left the room because I shouted at him.
   B When I shouted at him he left the room. ☐
   C When I was shouting at him he left the room. ☐

6 Past continuous or past perfect
Core grammar
Read these stories about failures. Change the verbs in bold either to the past continuous or the past perfect.

1. **The least successful animal rescue**
   In 1978 the firefighters in Britain went on strike. The Army began to do the work instead. On 14 January they were called out by an old lady. Her cat (**climb**) _____ a tree and couldn't get down. They arrived quickly and rescued the cat. The grateful old lady invited them for tea. Some time later, while they (**drive**) _____ away, they ran over the cat and killed it.

2. **The greatest mathematical error**
   The Mariner I space probe was launched from Cape Canaveral on 28 July 1962. It was expected to go to Venus. However, after four minutes it fell out of the sky into the Atlantic Ocean. Scientists later discovered that someone (**leave**) _____ out a minus sign (-) in the computer program. This minus sign cost £4,280,000 pounds.

3. **The least successful handcuffing**
   In 1978 a British judge (**try**) _____ a burglar. The police (**take**) _____ a pair of handcuffs from him when they caught him. The judge wanted to show how handcuffs worked. A lawyer told him not to, but he ignored him and fixed one handcuff round his wrist. Then he discovered that the police (**not find**) _____ the keys. The court case was stopped while the judge went to see a blacksmith.

4. **The slowest bank robber.**
   A robber in Malta took 3,000 new banknotes from the Bank of Valetta. He then crossed the street and waited for a bus. After 15 minutes a policeman arrested him. The policeman (**become**) _____ suspicious because the robber (**hold**) _____ the banknotes in his hands.

5. **The worst university boat race.**
   By 1984 Oxford and Cambridge (**win**) _____ the same number of races. Also, each of them had (**sink**) _____ three times (Cambridge, 1859 and 1978; Oxford, 1925 and 1951, and both in 1912). However, in 1984 Cambridge did something completely new. They managed to sink before the race began. Twenty minutes from the start they rowed into a boat that someone (**tie**) _____ up. Their boat broke in half.

7 can for logical possibility
Grammar extension
Each sentence below has **can** and another modal. Choose the more suitable modal and underline it.

When **can** is the correct choice, its meaning is logical possibility, not ability or permission.

1. There's somebody at the door – who **can/may** it be at this time of night.

2. She **can/must** be mad to take that job.

3. Using your mobile phone while driving **can/should** cause an accident.

4. Before you start with this firm you **can/have to** have a medical examination. It's compulsory.

5. OK, we lost the game but it **can/may** be a good thing. They'll probably sack the manager.

UNIT 12 Finding Work

6 You really **can/must** see your doctor about this. It's affecting your work and the boss is losing patience.

7 I know it's a good plan but I'm still worried. Sometimes things **can/should** go wrong and it's nobody's fault.

8 He's a successful TV presenter and he proves that people with disabilities **can/have to** get to the top.

9 'You **can/should** get out more – you're looking stressed.' 'I know, but I'm so busy these days.'

10 Think of a person you know – it **can/must** be a relative or a friend ... or anybody. Now imagine ...

8 Jobs

Vocabulary

The words in the box make up pairs in the same area of work. Put them together. Use your dictionary if you need help.

> camera(wo)man   chef   computer programmer
> detective   editor   film director   judge
> flight attendant   interpreter   lawyer
> model   nun   photographer   pilot
> police(wo)man   priest   reporter
> software designer   translator   waiter/waitress

Example: banker   bank clerk

9 Writing

Look at these pictures:

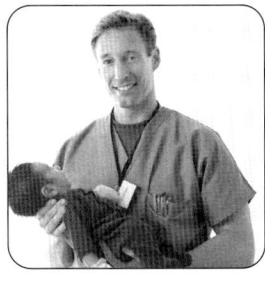 

Midwife   Soldier

Plumber   Au pair

House husband   Pilot

Are there jobs that only men or women should do? Which of these jobs do you think you could do? Think about the jobs above, and any others, and write your ideas here.

Finding Work UNIT 12

10 Pronunciation

Diphthongs: eɪ p<u>ay</u>   əʊ g<u>o</u>   aɪ m<u>y</u>   aʊ h<u>ow</u>   ɔɪ t<u>oy</u>

Look at this sentence:

əʊ → aʊ   Laura phoned her youngest son in the cupboard.

It's possible – maybe Laura was in the cupboard, or her youngest son was in the cupboard – but maybe unlikely. Look for a word in the sentence with the diphthong əʊ – **phoned**. Change the sound to əʊ – **found**:

              found

əʊ → aʊ   Laura ~~phoned~~ her youngest son in the cupboard.

Now it makes more sense.

Look at the sentences below. In each one, change a diphthong in one of the words to make the sentence more likely.

1 aɪ → ɔɪ   They bought the baby some ties for its first birthday.

2 eɪ → aɪ   Sam's a bit busy – he has to tape some letters.

3 əʊ → aʊ   There are some very expensive hoses in this street.

4 aɪ → eɪ   The job isn't much fun but the pie is good.

5 aʊ → əʊ   Nargis slept on the couch all the way to Glasgow.

6 ɔɪ → aɪ   Three t-shirts for six pounds – that's a good boy.

7 aɪ → eɪ   There are only two lines on this motorway.

8 eɪ → aɪ   He's earning pails of money in London.

9 aʊ → əʊ   The butcher bound the shoulder of lamb for me.

UNIT 13
At Work

1 Verbs followed by **to + verb** or **verb + -ing**.

Core grammar

In each sentence, change the verb in brackets to its **to** or **–ing** form. Write it on the line.

1 I'd appreciate (**see**) _____ that report.
2 I didn't expect (**hear**) _____ from Ahmed so soon.
3 I'm learning (**use**) _____ the new computer system.
4 Lorna keeps (**miss**) _____ department meetings.
5 I'd suggest (**get**) _____ a technician to have a look at this.
6 Saskia doesn't seem (**want**) _____ a promotion.
7 I don't want to risk (**invest**) _____ any more money in this company.
8 We can't afford (**hire**) _____ any more workers.
9 I want us to finish (**discuss**) _____ this by three o'clock.
10 We appear (**have**) _____ a problem here.

2 Verbs followed by **to + verb** or **verb + -ing**.

Core grammar

Choose between the two verbs in **bold** in each sentence.

1 Will you **finish/want** having lunch soon?
2 She **keeps/seems** to have health problems.
3 I'm going to **ask/suggest** the boss to send me on a training course.
4 You should **avoid/offer** speaking to Ronnie.
5 Hannah **appears/avoids** to do a lot of work.
6 Why don't you **offer/suggest** to take on more staff?
7 Charlie **keeps/pretends** getting angry with the trainees.
8 Asif **dislikes/wants** to work on the night shift.

3 Verbs followed by **to + verb** or **verb + -ing**.

Core grammar

Each sentence 1–6 has three verbs together. Change the second and third ones to their **to** or **–ing** forms and write them on the lines below.

Example:

Zoe **suggested offer pay** for the meal.
offering to pay

1 He **pretends want find** a job but he doesn't really.
   _____
2 This **involves agree do** a lot of evening work.
   _____
3 I've **given up try like** the new boss.
   _____
4 She **decided ask go** to the conference.
   _____
5 Marina **appears avoid do** all the difficult jobs.
   _____
6 Alan **seems expect earn** a lot of money.
   _____

At Work UNIT 13

4 Verbs followed by **verb+ing** or **to+verb** with a change in meaning.

Grammar extension

Choose the correct form of each verb in **bold**.

1 I forgot **posting/to post** the letter. It's still in my pocket.

2 Olive tried **passing/to pass** her driving test five times.

3 Roman really regrets **hitting/to hit** the traffic warden – because he went to prison for it.

4 This job means **moving/to move** to London.

5 I remember the car **leaving/to leave** the road but nothing after that.

6 He started as an office boy and went on **becoming/to become** the CEO.

7 I like **seeing/to see** the dentist every six months or so.

8 We stopped **visiting/to visit** my brother on the way back from France last week.

5 Verbs followed by **verb+ing** or **to+verb** with a change in meaning.

Grammar extension

Look at these workplace notices. On each line write a verb from the box in its **to** or **–ing** form

> bring   hand in   leave   play
> risk   say   stop   work

1
> The management regrets _____ that the canteen is closed today due to problems with the water supply.

2
> Please stop _____ dirty cups in the sink.
> Wash them and put them back in the cupboard.
> Zarina

3
> Do you like _____ golf?
> The staff golf club welcomes new members.
> Contact Steve in Accounts.

4
> Part-time staff.
> Remember _____ your pay claim by Friday 24th.

5
> DON'T FORGET _____
> A DISH FOR THE STAFF LUNCH ON FRIDAY.

6
> SMOKEFREE
> Trying _____ smoking?
> **Free** Smoking Helpline:
> 0800 022 4 332
> 7 Days a week,
> 7am to 11pm.
> *Here to help you!*

7
> Do you want to go on _____ here for ever? Join the staff lottery syndicate – your chance to win millions!
> See Cheryl in the Print Room.

8
> Entering this area without a safety helmet means _____ your life. Make sure you are wearing yours.

55

UNIT 13 At Work

6 Verbs joined with *to* or *–ing*.

Grammar extension

For each sentence, write the correct form of the two verbs in bold. Make changes for tense when you have to.

1 'I'm living on salad and fruit juice just now.' 'Are you (**try/lose**) _____ weight?'

2 Jason introduced me to Manfred. I didn't know who he was. I completely (**forget/meet**) _____ him at Kate's wedding last year.

3 Helen (**try/cycle**) _____ to work for a while. She enjoyed it but stopped when the weather got cold.

4 After she finished her business course she (**go on/start**) _____ her own company.

5 I was in Carlisle last week. I (**stop/have**) _____ lunch there on the way to Manchester.

6 I really (**regret/call**) _____ him an idiot – it was unfair. True, but unfair.

7 I (**like/see**) _____ my dentist every six months or so.

8 'Do you (**remember/tell**) _____ me about Janet's divorce last night?' 'Yes, I didn't (**mean/say**) _____ anything about it but I got a bit annoyed.'

7 Phrasal verbs with *get*

Vocabulary

In each sentence there are two words after **get**. Decide which is the correct one.

1 I want to do that training course. I think it'll help me to get **ahead/along**.

2 It's quite a serious illness but he's young and he's fit – he'll get **down to/over** it.

3 My dad's quite old now and he doesn't get **about/ahead** so much.

4 He stole money from the company and got **away with/over** it for years before they caught him.

5 I've got a cat and a dog but they don't get **along/by**.

6 OK, I made a mistake – I'm sorry. Now stop getting **about/at** me all the time.

7 This company's trying to do too many things and we're losing money. We need to shut down some of our operations and get **away with/back to** what we do best.

8 You've been wasting time all morning. When are you going to get **back to/down to** some work?

9 'Do we need more milk?' 'No, there isn't so much but I think we'll get **along/by**.'

8 Job titles

Vocabulary

Write one word from the box on each line to make job titles.

> auxiliary   chef   collector   driver
> engineer   executive   lecturer   mechanic
> nurse   officer   porter   programmer
> servant   teacher

taxi _____

police _____

school _____

mechanical _____

registered _____

kitchen _____

refuse _____

sous _____

university _____

marketing _____

motor _____

nursing _____

civil _____

computer _____

At Work UNIT 13

9 Writing

You have a friend who is a Career Development Officer. She is collecting descriptions of different jobs in your area, so that people can see if they want to do them. She asks you to write a description of a job.

Think of a job you do or you have done – or you would like to do.

Write its name here: _____

Now write something on each of the lines:

Good things about this job: _____
_____
_____

Bad things about this job: _____
_____
_____

Would you recommend this job to another person?
yes/no

Say why/why not. _____
_____

Now write a description of the job.

Job title: _____
_____
_____
_____
_____
_____
_____
_____
_____

10 Pronunciation

ɑː p<u>ar</u>t ɔː c<u>or</u>n ɜː th<u>ir</u>d ɪə d<u>ear</u> eə f<u>air</u>
θ <u>th</u>in ð <u>th</u>is ʃ <u>sh</u>ip

RP speakers don't say the **/r/** sound before consonants or at the end of words. Instead, they use a long vowel or a diphthong. The words below are written in the phonemic symbols that an RP speaker would use. Write them in normal spelling.

Example:

    k ɑː   *car* _____

1   m ɔː   _____
2   f ɑː   _____
3   b ɔː   _____
4   s ɜː   _____
5   h ɪə   _____
6   n ɪə   _____
7   ð eə   _____
8   k eə   _____
9   h ɑː t   _____
10   f ɑː m   _____
11   ʃ ɔː t   _____
12   b ɔː n   _____
13   ɜː θ   _____
14   w ɜː d   _____

UNIT 14
About Work

1 get used to

Core grammar

Decide which sentence beginnings **1–6** go with which ends **a–g**.

1	I'm	a	get used to working for them?
2	Have the new students	b	used to starting work so early?
3	Do you think you'll	c	to get used to this new software.
4	Michelle got	d	got used to the food yet?
5	I was just getting	e	getting used to the night shift.
6	Did he get	f	used to the job when they fired me.
7	I need	g	used to driving on the left very quickly.

2 used to, be/get used to

Core grammar

Choose the correct form of **used to**, **be used to** or **get used to** in each of these sentences.

1 We **used to/were used to** live in Pakistan.

2 Mr Summers **used to/'s getting used to** work for our main competitors.

3 She **used to/'s used to** working in Glasgow now.

4 It rains a lot in Manchester but the local people are **used to/getting used to** it.

5 He doesn't like the job much but he **used to/'s getting used to** it.

6 It's taking her a long time to **used to/get used to** the new house.

7 I **used to/'m used to** earn a higher salary.

8 The workers are slowly **used to/getting used to** the new production system.

9 I **used to/'m used to** a higher salary.

10 She **didn't use to/hasn't got used to** drive much before she changed jobs.

3 Active to passive

Core grammar

Rewrite these active sentences as passives. Don't use **by ...** in the passive sentence if it is unnecessary.

1 A truck hit my car.
   _____

2 Machines now do this work.
   _____

3 They fixed your computer.
   _____

4 The Health Minister opened the new hospital.
   _____

5 They invented a new process last year.
   _____

6 Somebody took the book from my bag.
   _____

7 We ask you not to smoke in here.
   _____

8 The police have arrested her brother.
   _____

9 They filmed the interview for the 6 o'clock news.
   _____

10 Do people still speak Irish?
   _____

4 Active and passive

Core grammar

In each pair of sentences, the first is active and the second is passive. Choose the better sentence in each pair. Write a tick (✔) on one of the lines.

1. a Joanne has had a baby. ___
   b A baby has been born to Joanne. ___

2. a My brother has just got a new job. ___
   b A new job has just been got by my brother. ___

3. a Some people saw an unusual bird in Orkney yesterday. ___
   b An unusual bird was seen in Orkney yesterday. ___

4. a Pytor drank three cups of coffee before he went to work. ___
   b Three cups of coffee were drunk by Pytor before he went to work. ___

5. a My friend Elham's mother gave birth to her in Khartoum. ___
   b My friend Elham was born in Khartoum. ___

6. a Someone killed Osman's grandfather in the First World War. ___
   b Osman's grandfather was killed in the First World War. ___

7. a The car wouldn't start so I took the bus to work. ___
   b The car wouldn't start so the bus was taken by me to work. ___

8. a The goalkeeper got hurt and people carried him off the field. ___
   b The goalkeeper got hurt and was carried off the field. ___

UNIT 14 About Work

5 Passive verbs

Grammar extension

Read the contract below. On each line **1–6**, write the passive form of one verb from the box

> appoint   employ   issue   notify
> provide   recognise

Moredun College
Braehead Avenue
Dumfries
DH1 1PX
United Kingdom

t +44 (0)1387 0247878
f +44 (0)1387 0247879

Zaida Ashraf
47 Comyn Street
Annan
DG12 5AD

Statement of main particulars of employment

Temporary Lecturer

This document is **1** _____ in accordance with the requirements of the Employment Rights Act 1996.

1 EMPLOYMENT DETAILS

a) Name of Employer: The Board of Management of Moredun College
b) Name of employee: Zaida Ashraf
c) Effective Date of Appointment: 7 September 2009
d) Date of issue of this Statement of Particulars: 16 August 2009
e) You are **2** _____ to a fixed-term contract, which will terminate on 25.09.09.

2 JOB TITLE

You are **3** _____ in the post of Temporary Lecturer in the Computing Department, reporting to the Head of Department, Computing, unless you are otherwise **4** _____ by the College.

3 PLACE OF WORK

You are employed at the College site at Braehead Avenue, Dumfries, DG1 1PX.

4 RECOGNITION OF PREVIOUS SERVICE

Continuous service with Moredun College and/or another local authority is **5** _____ when establishing entitlements to:

- Sickness allowances
- Holidays
- Maternity, Paternity, Adoption and Parental Benefits
- Redundancy payment
- The right to claim unfair dismissal
- All other statutory entitlements which are **6** _____ under the Employment Rights Act 1996.

About Work UNIT 14

6 Present continuous, present perfect and modal passives

Grammar extension

Choose the correct form in **bold** in each of the sentences.

1 I'm sorry – that job's already **being/been** taken. We appointed someone yesterday.
2 When do you think the repairs can **be/being** finished?
3 I may **be/have** finished the job by ten o'clock.
4 It's quiet today because some of the new staff **are being/have been** trained at head office.
5 I don't know the decision. I expect I'll **be/been** told tomorrow.
6 Astrid may **be/have** chosen a team leader.
7 Elsa may **be/have** appointed team leader.
8 OK, the circuit's **being/been** fixed. You can switch the electricity back on.

7 Phrasal verbs with *set*

Write one of the phrasal verbs with **set** on each line below. Make changes for tense and person.

> set about   set aside   set in
> set off   set up   set upon

1 We need to get the new office block finished before the winter _____.
2 He was _____ by a couple of guys on the way home last night. They beat him up and took his wallet and his mobile.
3 It's an important meeting and it might go on for a while. We'd better _____ two hours for it.
4 We're _____ a small committee to discuss the new health and safety regulations.
5 This project is very important and it's quite urgent so let's _____ it now.
6 Put that cigarette out – this place is full of chemicals. You might _____ an explosion.

8 *work* in idioms

Vocabulary

Lucy and Sanjeev meet in the company restaurant. Read their conversations. They use a number of idioms with the word **work** in them. For each one, choose between the two words in **bold**. Use your dictionary and make sure you understand the meaning of each idiom.

Lucy Hi Sanjeev – how are you?

Sanjeev Oh, hi Lucy – OK, I suppose. Yourself?

Lucy I'm fine. You do look a bit tired, you know.

Sanjeev I'm totally exhausted, actually. I've been working like a **dog/donkey** this week.

Lucy Oh – why?

Sanjeev It's this new contract. Everything's got to be ready to go tomorrow. We started late and we've been working against the clock. And, as usual, I've got to do the **donkey/horse** work – some of my colleagues are useless.

Lucy That's bad – mind you, it's the same in my department. It really annoys me when I'm working my fingers to the **bone/hand** and they're just chatting.

Sanjeev Yes, but you've got a more interesting job than mine. Where were you last week – the Bahamas?

Lucy Well, someone had to go and I was the best qualified. It was nice, though. The hotel was great – lovely swimming pool.

Sanjeev Huh! **Fine/Nice** work if you can get it.

Lucy Well, next week won't be so good. I have to go to Moscow and it'll be freezing cold at this time of year. Also, it's a pretty tough contract – there are three other firms competing for it.

Sanjeev Sounds like you'll have your work **cut/laid** out for you.

Lucy Yeah – that's the other side of things. I get to go to the Bahamas but they often ask me to do the **dirty/tough** work. For example, I have to sack one of the trainees tomorrow – she's completely useless.

UNIT 14 About Work

Sanjeev That sort of thing's all in a **day's/week's** work for you, though. You've done it before.

Lucy It's still difficult. The best thing is just to call them into the office and make **quick/short** work of it. Just say they're fired and explain why.

Sanjeev Well, someone has to do it and isn't your fault if they can't do the job. Anyway, I'll have to go. I have to get **down/up** to work again. Nice seeing you.

Lucy You too. Have fun.

Sanjeev Yeah, sure.

9 Writing

Think of three jobs you could never do. This may be because you think they're immoral, unpleasant or just very boring. Write their names here:

_____

_____

_____

Now write about why you could never do these jobs.

_____
_____
_____
_____
_____
_____
_____
_____
_____
_____
_____
_____

10 Pronunciation

Write each sentence under one of the stress patterns below. The first one is done for you.

~~Bob needs a break.~~   Write a letter.   It's not my job.   Fung's not here.

Where do you work?   Adam likes you.   Help me print it.   Pay them now.

Where's her desk?   The boss is mad.   Send him a text.   He's gone to France.

● • ●   ● • • ●   ● • • ●   • ● • ●

_____   _____   Bob needs a break.   _____
_____   _____   _____   _____
_____   _____   _____   _____
_____   _____   _____   _____

UNIT 15

Joining a Course

1 Sentences with *if*

Core grammar

Add *if* to one of the clauses below and *'ll* or *will* to the other to make sentences.

Write them on the lines. The first one has been done for you.

I go to university	I pass my exams
I'll go to university if I pass my exams.	

1 You give me the data / I write the report

2 The rain stops / We go to the park

3 I give Mr Hassan the information / I see him.

4 I have enough money / I buy a new jacket

5 Naria needs books / She get them from the library

6 You enjoy that course / You take it

7 You fill in this form / I process your application

8 I go for a swim / I have time tomorrow

2 Sentences with *if*

Core grammar

Put together the first parts (**1–9**) and the second parts (**a–i**) to make complete sentences.

1	If it doesn't rain tomorrow	a	you'll be safer in the water.
2	If you'll just take a seat	b	I'm going to be very angry.
3	If you don't come to the class	c	we can invite Ewan instead.
4	If you must smoke	d	I'll see if Mr Harris is free.
5	If you want a copy of the recipe	e	she'll probably pass the exam.
6	If Damien isn't coming to the dinner	f	send an e-mail to this address.
7	If you can swim	g	we can go mountain-biking.
8	If he's crashed my car	h	I may give your place to another student.
9	If she's been studying	i	please do it outside.

3 *if* or *when*

Core grammar

Complete these sentences with *if* or *when* and the correct form of a verb from the box.

> come   end   give   have   leave
> pass   throw   try

1 ____ I'm 16 I'm going to ____ school.

2 I'll be surprised ____ they ____ Moira the job.

3 We'll go camping ____ the summer ____.

4 ____ you don't get better marks you won't ____ the course.

63

UNIT 15 Joining a Course

5 _____ he doesn't shut up I'm going to _____ something at him.

6 We'll have to _____ something else _____ this doesn't work.

7 You'll _____ more freedom _____ you're older.

8 _____ the course _____ I'll have to look for a job.

4 Present perfect continuous

Core grammar

Put together the first sentence (**1–10**) and the second one (**a–j**) that each speaker says.

1 'My hands are covered with oil.
2 'Philip's a bit worried about his job.
3 'There's flooding in Yorkshire.
4 'I've got a really sore back.
5 'There's something wrong with the baby.
6 'I'm going to shoot that dog.
7 'Paula's given up playing rugby.
8 'Elise and James are going to break up.
9 'I'm not going shopping today.
10 'My eyes are full of tears.

a I've been spending too much recently.'
b She's been getting hurt too much.
c He's been seeing another woman.
d He's been crying for hours.'
e I've been digging the garden.
f I've been chopping onions.'
g I've been working on the car.'
h It's been raining for days.'
i He's been phoning me all week.'
j It's been barking all night.'

5 Present perfect continuous

Core grammar

Use the information provided to write a sentence in the present perfect continuous.

It started raining last night. It's still raining.
<u>It's been raining since last night.</u>

1 That man is watching me. He started doing it ten minutes ago. _____

2 Juliet's eyes are red and her hankie's wet.
_____

3 I came here twenty minutes ago. I'm still waiting to be served.
_____

4 Viktor has a black eye and a cut lip.
_____

5 They started travelling yesterday morning. They haven't arrived yet.
_____

6 Mark fell asleep on the couch two hours ago.
_____

7 I began to read this book a month ago.
_____

8 I've spoken many times to the boss about this over the past few weeks.
_____

6 Present perfect or present perfect continuous

Core grammar

Choose the better form of the verb in each sentence below.

1 Sarra's **lived/been living** in Britain all her life.

2 She's **told/been telling** them about this problem for weeks but they won't listen.

3 I'll speak to Veysel about it – he's just **arrived/been arriving**.

4 Joe has **worked/been working** for the company for 36 years.

5 Keira's upset about something – she looks like she's **cried/been crying**.

6 Get a mop – Omer's **dropped/been dropping** a cup of tea on the floor.

7 It looks like we're going to win – Murray's just **scored/been scoring** another goal.

8 What happened to your face? Have you **fought/been fighting** again?

9 I've **sent/been sending** emails about this for over a month and I'm getting nowhere.

7 Present simple with or without *will*

Grammar extension

In the sentences below, write a verb in each space in the **present simple** or with *will*.

1 When you ____ home, give me a ring. *(get)*

2 I can't talk now. I ____ to him as soon as the class is over. *(speak)*

3 Temel ____ to that café every day after classes ____. *(go) (finish)*

4 When I ____ school I ____ abroad. *(leave) (go)*

5 I don't want to go home yet. I ____ until the film ____. *(wait) (end)*

6 I think he ____ home before you ____. *(go) (arrive)*

7 My aunt ____ Capri. She ____ there until she ____. *(love) (live) (die)*

8 After Lim ____ her course, she ____ back to China. *(finish) (go)*

8 Education idioms

Vocabulary

Match the verbs (**1–10**) with the rest of these idioms (**a–j**). Then write one number and one letter before each meaning below. The first one is done for you.

1	cover	a	aloud
2	draw	b	with flying colours
3	drop out of	c	off campus
4	~~have~~	d	your way through college/university
5	learn	e	a lot of ground
6	live	f	a blank
7	pass	g	by heart
8	put	h	college/university
9	read	i	your thinking cap on
10	work	j	~~your nose in a book~~

_4_ _j_ Be reading a book.

___ ___ Complete a lot of material in a class or course.

___ ___ Do a job to help pay for your college/university expenses.

___ ___ Look for information but fail to find it.

___ ___ Live in a different place, away from the grounds of a university.

___ ___ Memorize something so you can repeat it without thinking.

___ ___ Pass a test or exam with a high score.

___ ___ Read something so that other people can hear you.

___ ___ Start thinking in a serious way.

___ ___ Stop attending college/university.

UNIT 15 Joining a Course

9 Phrasal verbs with *put*

Match the phrasal verbs in the box with the more formal verbs below. Write one phrasal verb on each line.

> put across   put by   put forward
> put in for   put off   put on   put out
> put up   put up with

1 apply for   _____
2 begin to wear   _____
3 build   _____
4 explain   _____
5 extinguish   _____
6 postpone   _____
7 save for later   _____
8 suggest a plan   _____
9 tolerate   _____

10 Writing

Elena is a student from the Ukraine. She's studying in Edinburgh. The sentences below come from an e-mail from Elena to her friend Sandra – but they're in the wrong order. Write the letters **a–k** in the correct order on the lines below. Use the words in **bold** to help you.

○ Send

To: _____
Subject: _____

Hi Sandra,

a I've got some **friends** now.
b How's everything with **you**?
c OK, **I'll get back to you** soon.
d There is one guy ... his name's **Liam**.
e **I'm** still enjoying life here in Edinburgh.
f **He's** from Dublin – and I know you want to know **what he looks like**.
g Anyway, **there's no hurry** – I'd rather wait for a while and see how it goes.
h **It's not all bad news** because I think **they're not getting on very well** at the moment.
i OK, I fancy him quite a lot and maybe he fancies me a bit – but **he has a girlfriend** back in Ireland.
j There's **Weilan** from China and **Lorna** – she's English, and some others, but no **boyfriend** yet.
k Well, he's a year older than me, and **a little taller** and he's got **brown hair** and **grey eyes** – but there's **one problem**.

Love,

Elena

____ ____ ____ ____ ____ ____ ____ ____ ____ ____ ____

Joining a Course UNIT 15

Now write an email to a friend. Tell them about your life at the moment. Write about your studies or work, or both. Write about people you've met recently and how you feel about your life at the moment.

11 Pronunciation

When people use text, text messaging, Internet chat rooms or e-mails they often write abbreviations. Look at these:

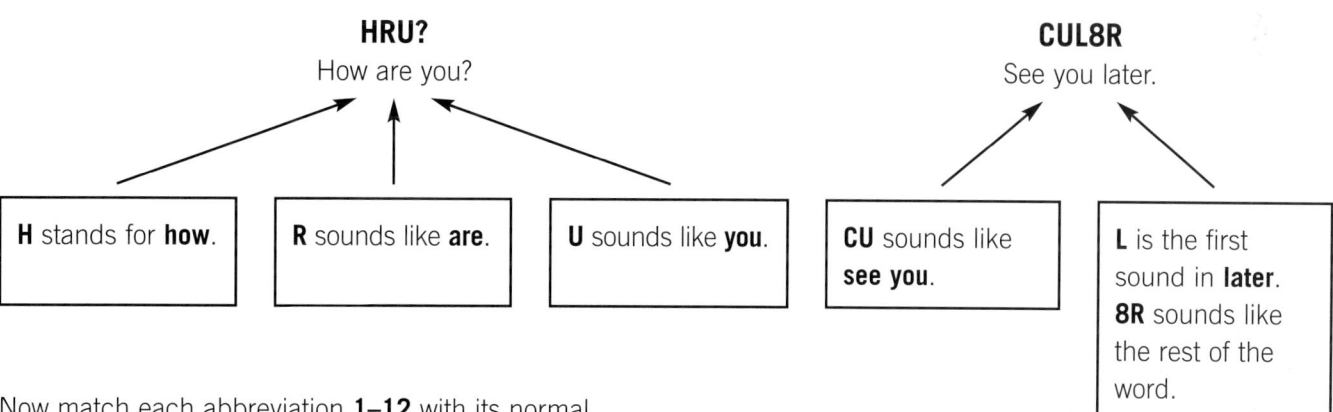

Now match each abbreviation **1–12** with its normal English form **a–l**.

1	ASAP	a	Have a nice day
2	B4	b	Good to see you
3	BFN	c	Great
4	BRB	d	Be right back
5	G2CU	e	Thank God it's Friday
6	GR8	f	See you in the morning
7	H2CUS	g	Are you okay?
8	HAND	h	Before
9	LOL	i	Bye for now
10	RUOK?	j	As soon as possible
11	SUITM	k	Lots of love/Laughing out loud
12	TGIF	l	Hope to see you soon

UNIT 16
Studying

1 2nd conditionals

Core grammar

Change the verbs in bold to make second conditional sentences. Use **would** where necessary.

1 If I (**have**) the money I (**help**) you but I don't so I can't.

2 She (**get**) better marks if she (**do**) a bit more work.

3 If Franz (**be**) in his office I (**speak**) to him but he's on a plane.

4 I (**buy**) more things if I (**have**) as much money as he has.

5 I (**not take**) that course if I (**be**) you.

6 If he (**drive**) any faster he (**go**) backwards.

7 You (**earn**) more money if you (**did**) some training courses.

8 If you (**stop**) eating chips every day you (**lose**) weight.

2 1st and 2nd conditionals

Core grammar

Change the verbs in bold to make 1st or 2nd conditional sentences. Use **will** or **would** where necessary.

1 I really can't help. I don't know what you should do. If I (**know**) I (**tell**) you.

2 OK, if I (**finish**) this essay before eight o'clock I (**call**) you and we can go out.

3 He died twenty years ago. If he (**be**) alive today he (**be**) over ninety.

4 It isn't a good idea. If it (**be**) we (**invest**) some money in it.

5 If you (**see**) Loretta (**you give**) her this parcel?

6 If he (**be**) here I'm sure he (**fix**) the problem but he's in Berlin today.

7 Let's buy a lottery ticket together. If we (**win**) we (**share**) the money.

8 Give Susan a ring. If she (**have**) time I'm sure she (**help**) you.

3 1st or 2nd conditional

Core grammar

Choose the better verb form.

1 If I **have/had** a billion pounds ....

2 If I **am/was** the cleverest person in the world ...

3 If the interest rate **goes/went** up next month ...

4 I haven't seen him for 20 years, but if he **is/was** still alive ...

5 If it **rains/rained** in Glasgow tomorrow ...

6 If I **am/was** taller than I am ...

7 If Shakespeare **is/was** alive today ....

8 If Ahmed **is/was** late for class again ...

9 If I **am/was** you ...

10 If you **see/saw** a raincoat in the sale ...

4 If I/he/she/it were ...

Grammar extension

In formal English, we often use **were** instead of **was** with **I, he, she** or **it**. Use the information below and write a new sentence with **were** on each line.

Example:

I'm not him. I don't know what to do.
If I were him I'd know what to do.

1 Bridget isn't here. She won't help us.
___

2 I'm not a cat. I don't chase mice.
___

3 I'm not as rich as my uncle. I don't live in a big house.
___

Studying UNIT 16

4 It's not possible. We won't do it.
   _____

5 I'm not tall. I don't play basketball.
   _____

6 He isn't good at the job. We won't keep him on.
   _____

5 Past simple in unreal present/future time

Grammar extension

Some of the verbs in bold below need the past form. Others need the present form or **to/-ing**. Write each verb in the correct form.

1 It's time you (**get**) _____ a job.

2 Adrian wants (**know**) _____ what to do with the old books.

3 If only I (**know**) _____ the answers to these questions.

4 Suppose Chisako (**take**) _____ that course, what would she do after it?

5 I hope he (**see**) _____ Stefana at the party tonight.

6 I wish I (**have**) _____ a better brain!

7 Let's (**go**) (**see**) _____ a film tonight.

8 I'd rather we (**not go**) _____ to Glasgow tomorrow.

9 I thought Sam (**know**) _____ how to do this but it's obvious he hasn't a clue.

10 When she (**finish**) _____ (**answer**) _____ her emails, ask her (**come**) _____ and (**see**) _____ me.

6 Real and unreal use of *modals*

Grammar extension

Choose the better modal in each of the sentences below.

1 We **will/would** accept you onto the course but unfortunately all the places are taken.

2 Sometimes, in those days, I **may/might** have time to play tennis after work.

3 I **might/would** finish my project this week.

4 I **can/could** speak Urdu when I was young but I've forgotten most of it.

5 He'd lend us the money if he **could/would** but he doesn't have it.

6 **Could/might** you give me some help with these equations?

7 There **would/might** be a chance to see him on Thursday but I doubt it.

8 Before his grandmother died he **will/would** often visit her on Sundays.

9 I **can/could** perhaps ... just possibly ... go out with him but I'm a bit nervous about it.

7 Phrasal verbs with *look*

Write a suitable word on each line to make a phrasal verb with **look**.

Example:

   We don't know who stole the money. The police are looking *into* it.

1 Could you look _____ Walter Libarsky's number in the phone book? I want to give him a ring.

2 I'm going to look _____ on my sister on the way home. She had a baby last week.

3 Excuse me, I'm looking _____ Angela Mackay. Do you know if she's in?

4 I can't see you tonight. My parents are going out and I have to look _____ my little sister.

5 Just give me ten minutes to look _____ the shop. I want to see what they have.

6 'What are you looking _____ ?' 'Well, it's your new hairstyle – it's so ... different.'

7 Rene's first marriage was a disaster. She doesn't like to look _____ on it.

UNIT 16 Studying

8 American English

Vocabulary

The words in **bold** below are in American English. Change each one for one of the British English words in the box.

> aeroplane   autumn   bonnet   boot
> garden   holiday   junction   lever   luggage
> motorway   pavement   queue   trouser
> tyres   windscreen

George carried his **(1) baggage** _____ to the car and put it in the **(2) trunk** _____. He stood on the **(3) sidewalk** _____ and looked back across the front **(4) yard** _____ to his house. He had lived on Sefton Street now for over a year and this was his first **(5) vacation** _____. He reached into his **(6) pants** _____ pocket, pulled a cloth out and cleaned the **(7) windshield** _____. It was quite hot – the summer weather had lasted well into the **(8) fall** _____. He lifted the **(9) hood** _____ and checked the oil. Then he checked the **(10) tires** _____, got into the car and drove off. He turned left at the first **(11) intersection** _____ and drove onto the **(12) freeway** _____. He moved the gear **(13) shift** _____ and got the car into top gear. He was early because he didn't want to **(14) stand in line** _____ at the check-in desk. He felt tired but knew he could sleep on the **(15) airplane** _____. Life was getting better.

9 Writing

Think about education in Scotland, and in another country that you know. Write some ideas here:

In Scotland:

good things   bad things
_____   _____
_____   _____
_____   _____

In _____

good things   bad things
_____   _____
_____   _____
_____   _____

Now write about the two educational systems. Compare them. Which one do you think is better?

10 Pronunciation

This wordsquare has the names of 11 school subjects in phonemic script. Their names are horizontal → or vertical ↓. Write them on the lines in normal spelling. Use all the letters. The first one is done for you.

dʒ	ɪ	ɒ	g	r	ə	f	ɪ
h	b	aɪ	ɒ	l	ə	dʒ	ɪ
ɪ	ɪ	m	j	ʊ	z	ɪ	k
s	ŋ	f	r	e	n	ʃ	m
t	g	d	r	ɑː	m	ə	æ
ə	l	dʒ	ɜː	m	ə	n	θ
r	ɪ	s	aɪ	ə	n	s	s
ɪ	ʃ	f	ɪ	z	ɪ	k	s

music

iː	bean	ɜː	work	p	path	θ	broth	m	sum
ɪ	bin	ə	ago	b	bath	ð	brother	n	sun
e	pen	eɪ	pay	t	tie	s	bus	ŋ	sung
æ	ant	aɪ	pie	d	die	z	buzz	l	load
ɑː	aunt	əʊ	know	k	class	ʃ	sure	r	road
ɒ	cot	aʊ	now	g	glass	ʒ	measure	j	yet
ɔː	caught	ɔɪ	toy	f	few	tʃ	choke	w	wet
ʌ	cut	ɪə	here	v	view	dʒ	joke	h	high
ʊ	pull	eə	there						
uː	pool	ʊə	tour						

Answers

Unit 1

1
1 he's got
2 Have you got
3 She hasn't got
4 He's got
5 they've got
6 We've got
7 You haven't got
8 it's got

2
1 's/has got
2 hasn't got
3 haven't got
4 've/have got
5 haven't got
6 haven't got
7 hasn't got
8 haven't got
9 's/has got
10 've/have got

3
1 I have/'ve got
2 I have/'ve got
3 I haven't got
4 They have/'ve/He has/'s got
5 It has/'s got
6 She has/'s got
7 He has/'s got
8 He hasn't got
9 She has/'s got
10 has got

4

5
1 fourteen
2 thirteen
3 eleven
4 fifteen
5 twelve
6 thirty
7 eight
8 eighteen

6a

ending in -i	ending in -ish	ending in -ese
Iraqi	Finnish	Chinese
Kuwaiti	Swedish	Japanese
Pakistani	Scottish	Portuguese

ending in -an	ending in -ian	ending in -ean
American	Hungarian	Chilean
German	Iranian	Guinean
Mexican	Russian	Korean

6b
Cypriot
French
Greek
Dutch
Swiss

7
a Open answers
b rock

8
1 FLIPCHART
2 VIDEO RECORDER
3 HEADPHONES
4 CD PLAYER
5 WHITEBOARD
6 POWERPOINT PROJECTOR
7 DVD PLAYER
8 INTERACTIVE WHITEBOARD

Unit 2

1
1 has
2 washes
3 misses
4 teaches
5 enjoys
6 flies
7 watches
8 goes
9 argues
10 cries
11 is
12 catches
13 finishes
14 worries
15 tries

2
1 Her parents don't live far away.
2 Hannah doesn't eat meat.
3 These trousers aren't too big for me.
4 Mark doesn't walk to work.

Answers

5 I don't want a new bike.
6 My sister doesn't usually get up early.
7 Karen's isn't a good guitarist.
8 Mary and her boyfriend don't like that café.
9 My dog doesn't eat too much.
10 They don't make good food in this restaurant.

3
1 Does Elena live in that house?
2 Do you need an ambulance now?
3 Is Dave sorry about the mess?
4 Do they have this jacket in blue?
5 Does Josep drink tea?
6 Is Ana here now?
7 Does Marta play tennis on Saturdays?
8 Does Alessandra want more money?
9 Do Nasreen and Sandra often go shopping together?
10 Is Jan in London today?

4
1 Where do you live?
2 How do you get to work?
3 When do you start work?
4 How much do you earn?
5 Why do you like your job?
6 Who do you like in the shop?
7 Which day of the week do you like best?

5
1 Yes, they do.
2 No, it doesn't.
3 No, they don't.
4 No, he doesn't.
5 Yes, they do.
6 No, he doesn't.
7 Yes, it does.
8 No, it doesn't.

6
1 **They sunbathe** on the beach.
2 **He plays** football.
3 **She walks** in the hills.
4 **He swims** in the pool.
5 **She skis** in Italy.
6 **He plays** the piano.
7 **She teaches** in the college.
8 **She flies** a plane.

7
4 coming
5 swimming
6 studying
7 moving
8 biting
9 taking
10 sitting
11 choosing
12 getting
13 saving
14 beginning
15 writing
16 digging
17 caring
18 opening
19 arriving
20 hiding
21 meeting
22 riding
23 carrying
24 having
25 changing
26 running
27 crying
28 playing
29 driving
30 liking

8
1 's/is coming
2 are swimming
3 's/is sitting
4 are moving
5 's/is changing
6 's/is running
7 'r/are winning
8 'm/am opening
9 'm/am saving
10 're/are dying

9
'm/am sitting. 'm/am drinking. 's/is eating
Are you studying
'm/am not working. 'm/am sitting.
Are you watching
are winning.
'm/am writing
's/is enjoying
'm not going
're working

10
2 Is it raining?/isn't
3 Are you laughing?/m not
4 Are they watching?/are
5 Are you working?/am
6 Am I dreaming?/aren't
7 Are you coming?/aren't
8 Is it growing?/is
9 Is she singing?/is
10 Is he lying?/isn't
11 Is she talking?/isn't
12 Are you shopping?/are
13 Are they eating?/are
14 Are they going?/aren't

11 1 B 2 B 3 A 4 B 5 B 6 B 7 B 8 A 9 A 10 B

12
1 always rises
2 is always getting
3 always take
4 always take
5 'm always meeting
6 always watches
7 are always getting
8 's always buying
9 always go

13
1 knives
2 deer
3 mice
4 churches
5 buses
6 loaves
7 ladies
8 parties
9 potatoes
10 heroes

14
1 pair
2 officer/constable/sergeant, etc
3 cost
4 some
5 flights

Answers

6 money/savings
7 building
8 are

15
1 between
2 under
3 above
4 in front of, behind, beside

16
1 currency
2 receipt
3 reduced
4 change
5 cheque
6 credit card

17 1 b 2 f 3 a 4 d 5 c 6 e

19 1 ✔ 2 ✘ 3 ✔ 4 ✔ 5 ✘ 6 ✘ 7 ✔ 8 ✘ 9 ✔ 10 ✘
11 ✔ 12 ✘

Unit 3

1
1 much
2 a lot of
3 no
4 much
5 some
6 any
7 some
8 many

2

	countable	uncountable
1 flour		✔
2 wall	✔	
3 glass	✔	✔
4 flower	✔	
5 paper	✔	✔
6 meat		✔
7 coffee	✔	✔
8 song	✔	
9 music		✔
10 pizza	✔	✔

3
1 some
2 a
3 a
4 a
5 some
6 a
7 some
8 a
9 some
10 some

4
1 papers
2 glass
3 cakes
4 time
5 beer
6 chickens
7 beers
8 wood
9 cake
10 coffees

11 wood
12 times
13 coffee
14 glasses
15 paper
16 Chicken

5
1 am
2 are
3 isn't
4 don't
5 is
6 don't
7 do
8 doesn't

6
1 're/are painting's/is taking
2 're/are driving have
3 's/is he shouting
4 comes sits starts arrives
5 lives 's/is staying
6 take crack stir
7 'm/am cycling
8 does

7 1 ✔ 2 ✘ 3 ✘ 4 ✘ 5 ✔ 6 ✘ 7 ✔

8 1 d 2 e 3 c 4 a 5 f 6 b

10
••	nature	onion	petrol
••	control	mature	online
•●•	animal	instrument	recipe
•●•	annoying	instruction	recover

Unit 4

1
1 an the
2 the
3 a
4 0
5 the the
6 a
7 the
8 the
9 a
10 a

2

Scotland	___
England	___
Northern Ireland	___
Wales	___
Republic of Ireland	✔
Isle of Man	✔
North Sea	✔
Irish Sea	✔
Loch Lomond	___
Lake Windermere	___
River Tay	✔
River Severn	✔
River Thames	✔
Skye	___ (but we also say The Isle of Skye)
Lewis	___
Grampian Mountains	✔
Pentland Hills	✔

Answers

Southern Uplands ✔
Lake District ✔
Aberdeen ___
Edinburgh ___
London ___
Highland Region ___
Strathclyde Region ___
Firth of Forth ✔
English Channel ✔
Bristol Channel ✔

3 1 a 2 b 3 b 4 a 5 a 6 b 7 a

4
1 very
2 very
3 too
4 too
5 very
6 too
7 very
8 too

5
1 harbour, gangway, cabin, deck
2 station, platform, carriage, buffet
3 check-in, desk, flight, luggage, excess baggage, hand luggage

6
a Minimum speed
b Mini roundabout
c One way traffic
d Vehicles may pass on either side
e Road narrows on the right
f Wild animals
g No motor vehicles
h No stopping
i No U-turns
j No right turn

8
1 **a** BA graduate — **a** Bachelor of Arts graduate
2 **a** CIA agent — **a** Central Intelligence Agency agent
3 **an** ESOL student — **an** English for Speakers of Other Languages student
4 **an** IOU — **an** I Owe You
5 **a** JP — **a** Justice of the Peace
6 **an** MP — **a** Member of Parliament
7 **an** NHS hospital — **a** National Health Service hospital
8 **an** SQA assessment — **a** Scottish Qualifications Authority assessment
9 **a** UN conference — **a** United Nations conference
10 **a** WHO report — **a** World Health Organisation report

Unit 5

1
1 Would you like …?
2 Do you like ..?
3 Do you like ..?
4 Would you like …?
5 Do you like ..?
6 Would you like …?

2
1 Yes, I would./No, I wouldn't.
2 Yes, I do./No, I don't.
3 Yes, I would./No, I wouldn't.
4 Yes, I would./No, I wouldn't.
5 Yes, I do./No, I don't.
6 Yes, I would./No, I wouldn't.
7 Yes, I do./No, I don't.
8 Yes, I would./No, I wouldn't.

3
1 'Yes, wait a minute. OK, I**'ll have** the fish.'
2 'I hope so. She**'s going to get married** on Saturday.'
3 'OK, I**'ll go**.'
4 'Ten past? OK, I**'ll meet** you at the station.'
5 'I'm OK, but Jake**'s going to** fly to Paris tonight.'

4 1 a 2 b 3 a 4 a 5 b 6 a

5
1 Shall we have a coffee? ✔ — I'd prefer have tea. ___
  Shall we to have a coffee? ___ — I'd prefer tea. ✔
2 Let's going out tonight. ___ — I'd rather stay in. ✔
  Let's go out tonight. ✔ — I'd rather to stay in. ___
3 Let's have lunch. ✔ — I'm not hungry. I'd rather waiting. ___
  Let's having lunch. ___ — I'm not hungry. I'd rather wait. ✔
  OK – in about an hour? — Yes, I'd prefer to that. ___
  — Yes, I'd prefer that. ✔
4 Shall we watch a video? ✔ — I'd prefer not to. ✔
  Shall we watching a video? ___ — I'd prefer not. ___
5 Would you like a cake? ✔ — I'd rather a biscuit. ___
  Would you liking a cake? ___ — I'd rather have a biscuit. ✔

6 1 f 2 g 3 h 4 b 5 e 6 d 7 c 8 a

7 10, 4, 6, 15, 2, 14, 13, 9, 1, 7

8 1 tomato 2 mushroom 3 carrot, potato 4 lettuce, cabbage 5 onion 6 aubergine 7 sweetcorn

10 1 slam 2 sleep 3 sleeve 4 sneeze 5 snow 6 steady 7 stuff 8 stun 9 style 10 sweat

Unit 6

1
1 Cairo has **fewer** people than Karachi but **more** than Edinburgh.
2 Karachi gets **more** rain than Cairo but **less** than Edinburgh.
3 Of the three, Edinburgh has **the most** rain and Cairo has **the least**.
4 Edinburgh has **the fewest** people and Karachi has **the most**.

Answers

2
1. Noriko is as old as Fahad.
2. Fahad is older than Salima.
3. Noriko isn't as tall as Fahad.
4. Fahad is as tall as Salima.
5. Salima isn't as old as Fahad.
6. Salima is taller than Noriko.
7. Noriko is older than Salima.
8. Salima isn't as old as Noriko.
9. Salima is as tall as Fahad.
10. Salima is the youngest.
11. Noriko is the smallest.

3
1. as lucky as
2. as big as
3. as slim as
4. as difficult as

4
1. Celtic **play/plays** Aberdeen **on** Saturday 25th.
2. The next train **to** London **leaves/is at** 10 o'clock.
3. The restaurant **opens** tonight **at** 7.00.
4. Term 2 **ends/finishes on** Friday 31st March.
5. The Paris flight **arrives at** 14.45.
6. The sale **ends on** the 15th January.

5
1 ✗ 2 ✓ 3 ✗ 4 ✗ 5 ✓ 6 ✓ 7 ✗ 8 ✓ 9 ✓ 10 ✗

6
1. Susie **is having** lunch with Marcia tomorrow.
2. We have to go now. The film **starts** at seven o'clock.
3. **I'm not going out** with Bob tonight. I'm too tired.
4. When **does** her plane **arrive**?
5. **Are** they **getting** married soon?
6. The train **leaves** in an hour.
7. **Is** Alice **going** to London tomorrow?
8. Slow down – the shops **don't open** till nine.
9. I have to leave early – **I'm seeing** the doctor at four.
10. **Do** you **have** a test on Monday?

7
1 a ✗ b ✓
2 a ✓ b ✓
3 a ✗ b ✓
4 a ✗ b ✓
5 a ✓ b ✓
6 a ✓ b ✓
7 a ✗ b ✓
8 a ✗ b ✓

8

TV	cinema
~~article~~	film star
channel	~~game show~~
documentary	studio
soap opera	stuntman/woman
game show	**extra**

theatre	newspaper
~~extra~~	column
interval	editor
performance	~~playwright~~
stage	reporter
playwright	**article**

10
1. wa<u>l</u>k
2. autum<u>n</u>
3. <u>k</u>not
4. thum<u>b</u>
5. <u>w</u>rist
6. pa<u>l</u>m
7. resi<u>g</u>n
8. s<u>w</u>ord
9. de<u>b</u>t
10. <u>h</u>our
11. <u>g</u>host
12. cas<u>t</u>le
13. mus<u>c</u>le
14. s<u>c</u>ientific

Unit 7

1
1. straight
2. hard
3. well
4. late
5. widely
6. fast
7. friendly
8. luckily

2

verb	noun
play	player
act	action
collect	collection
agree	agreement
argue	argument

noun	adjective
fashion	fashionable
accident	accidental
music	musical
beauty	beautiful
help	helpful
child	childish
fool	foolish

adjective	verb
weak	weaken
wide	widen
equal	equalise
legal	legalise
modern	modernise

3
1. weaken
2. agreement
3. musical
4. argument
5. collection
6. widen
7. loosen
8. sharpen
9. childish
10. modernise

Answers

4
1. Tigers are faster than tortoises.
2. Curry is hotter than salad.
3. Aberdeen is colder than Paris.
4. Cars are more expensive than bicycles.
5. Motorways are wider than country roads.
6. Skiing is more dangerous than table tennis.
7. People are more intelligent than cats.
8. Horror films are more frightening than comedies.

5
1. ✔
2. ✘
3. ✘
4. ✔
5. ✘
6. ✔
7. ✘
8. ✘
9. ✔
10. ✘

6
1. do you do
2. I'm having
3. I don't feel
4. I'm phoning
5. He's scoring
6. Do you see
7. smells
8. don't want
9. hates
10. 's landing

7
1. half-brother
2. stepsister
3. stepbrother
4. stepfather
5. stepmother
6. half-sister
7. stepson
8. stepdaughters
9. stepdaughter
10. stepfather

8
1. faster
2. best
3. harder
4. worst
5. more fluently
6. better
7. more carefully
8. furthest/farthest, earliest
9. more sensitively

10
1. grate
2. plain
3. raise
4. steak
5. sale
6. steel
7. stationary
8. tale
9. wade
10. weight
11. leek
12. scent

Unit 8

1
1. Did you enjoy the film? Yes, I did.
2. Was she out last night? Yes, she was.
3. Did Anna apply for the job? No, she didn't.
4. Did Fraser go to China last year? Yes, he did.
5. Were you at the party? No, I wasn't
6. Were they at the same school? No, they weren't.

2
1. 'Where did they go? 'To the cinema.'
2. 'How much did it cost?' 'Seven pounds.'
3. 'Why did Imran not like the film?' 'It was quite violent.'
4. 'Why did they walk back to Baz's flat?' 'They missed the bus.'
5. 'When did they arrive?' 'At half-past eleven.'
6. 'What did they do after that?' 'They drank coffee.'

3
1. I didn't finish the coffee.
2. I didn't switch off the TV.
3. Marta didn't go to Rome.
4. I didn't drive to London.
5. I didn't have a holiday last year.
6. Nasreen didn't lie to me.
7. They didn't go for a drink.
8. We didn't meet in New York.

4

group 1
cost	cost	cost
let	let	let
put	put	out

group 2
become	became	become
come	came	come

group 3
buy	bought	bought
hear	heard	heard
mean	meant	meant
teach	taught	taught

group 4
choose	chose	chosen
freeze	froze	frozen
shake	shook	shaken

group 5
fly	flew	flown
grow	grew	grown
know	knew	known

group 6
drink	drank	drunk
sing	sang	sung
swim	swam	swum

5 1 a ✔ 2 a ✔ b ✔ 3 b ✔ 4 b ✔

6

politics	backbencher	secretary of state
restaurant	commis chef	kitchen porter
school	headteacher	principal teacher
local government	councillor	provost
army	captain	private
church	bishop	elder
company	director	shareholder
police	constable	inspector
hospital	anaesthetist	midwife
university	lecturer	professor
trade union	branch secretary	shop steward

Answers

8

	/t/	/d/	/ɪd/
hated	—	—	✔
decided	—	—	✔
rushed	✔	—	—
hoped	✔	—	—
ended	—	—	✔
saved	—	✔	—
closed	—	✔	—
picked	✔	—	—
grabbed	—	✔	—
landed	—	—	✔
coughed	✔	—	—
touched	✔	—	—
dodged	—	✔	—
wasted	—	—	✔
missed	✔	—	—

Unit 9

1
1. Can I
2. Can I use
3. Can I come
4. Can I bring
5. Can I walk on the grass?
6. Can I have

2 1 can, 2 may, 3 may not, 4 can't, 5 can, 6 may not, 7 may not, 8 can

3
1. can
2. can't
3. could
4. couldn't
5. could
6. can
7. can't
8. can't
9. could
10. couldn't

4
1. Could
2. Couldn't
3. mightn't
4. couldn't
5. could
6. could
7. might not
8. might

5
1. It might rain.
2. She might fall.
3. He might drop them.
4. He might miss/catch it.

6 1 alley 2 car park 3 zebra crossing 4 junction 5 railway bridge 6 fountain 7 crossroads 8 subway 9 harbour 10 taxi rank 11 pedestrian precinct 12 park 13 street market 14 pavement 15 roundabout 16 pier 17 parking meters

7
sunny
sunny intervals
black, low level cloud
light rain shower
heavy rain
sleet
hail
light snow
heavy snow
thundery shower

9
aeroplane
motorbike
passenger

demolish
location
recycling

ability
facilities
historical

economics
entertainment
conservation

Unit 10

1 1 sung, 2 broken, 3 thrown, 4 drunk, 5 woken, 6 drawn, 7 shone, 8 flown

2
1. 's/has finished
2. have come
3. 's/has visited
4. 've/have
5. 's/have
6. 've/have
7. have sent
8. has started

3
1. He hasn't left the country.
2. Has Mikel gone to play tennis?
3. Who have you spoken to?
4. I haven't finished my essay.
5. This hasn't happened before.
6. How long have you lived here?
7. Irina hasn't had lunch.
8. Have you seen that film before?
9. Why has he left?
10. I haven't met your sister.
11. Has the cat gone out?
12. Where has he gone?

4 1 gone 2 been 3 been 4 gone 5 been 6 gone 7 been 8 gone

5
1. took
2. saw
3. 's/has bought
4. 's/has gone
5. bought
6. 's/has just dropped
7. arrived
8. 've/have left
9. told

6 1a, 2b, 3a, 4a, 5b

Answers

7
1. She lived in Italy before she came here.
2. I think I've met him some time before.
3. ✔
4. ✔
5. When I was your age I spent a lot of money on clothes.
6. Who lived in that flat last year?
7. She's around here somewhere – I saw her five minutes ago.
8. ✔
9. Where did you go last night?
10. ✔

8 1 no 2 no 3 yes 4 no 5 yes 6 no 7 yes

9 1 a 2 a 3 b 4 b 5 a 6 b 7 a 8 b

10 1 a 2 a 3 b 4 a 5 b 6 a 7 b 8 b

11
1. I've been
2. I thought
3. I was
4. I got
5. it was
6. It rained
7. I arrived
8. it's rained
9. I had
10. I knew
11. I've never seen
12. I've never been
13. I've eaten
14. I've eaten

Hello _G'day_   Australia _Oz_
British _Pommy_   Tasmania _Tassie_

note: *Pommy*, along with *Pom*, is used by Australians for British people, e.g. 'He's a pommy/pom.' Nobody is sure how this term started.

12
1. ago
2. yet
3. for
4. ago
5. Since
6. for
7. yet
8. for
9. since
10. ago
11. since
12. yet

13
1. used to
2. m'/am used to
3. 's/is used to
4. used to
5. 's/is used to
6. 'm/am used to
7. used to
8. 'm/am used to
9. used to

14 1 a 2 d 3 j 4 c 5 f 6 b 7 e 8 i 9 h 10 g

16
θ	thing	teeth
ð	they	this
ʃ	machine	shop
ʒ	beige	usual
tʃ	chair	nature
dʒ	jam	urgent
ŋ	ankle	singer

Unit 11

1
1. 'Must you play your music so loud?'
2. 'You don't have to leave so early.'
3. 'Does she have to come with us?'
4. 'Why do you have to do that?'
5. 'Must they lose so many games?'
6. 'Do you really have to go to work today?'
7. 'She mustn't see him again.'
8. 'What must I do to be in the team?'
9. 'You mustn't talk in here.'
10. 'Where do I have to go now?'
11. 'I don't have to work.'
12. 'When do I have to finish this?'

2
1. have to
2. must
3. has to
4. have
5. must
6. have to
7. must
8. must
9. have to

3
1. must
2. should
3. should
4. must
5. should

4
1. have to
2. should
3. have to
4. must
5. must

5
1. a obligation
   b deduction
2. a obligation
   b deduction
3. a deduction
   b obligation
4. a obligation
   b deduction
5. a deduction
   b obligation
6. a deduction
   b obligation

Answers

6 1 bagpipes 2 piano 3 harp 4 guitar 5 clarinet
6 banjo 7 trumpet 8 harmonica/mouth organ 9 flute
10 drums

7 1 f 2 j 3 d 4 k 5 a 6 l 7 i 8 g 9 e 10 c 11 b
12 h

9
1 bone	cone	<u>gone</u>	phone
2 <u>does</u>	goes	hoes	toes
3 <u>con</u>	son	ton	won
4 catch	hatch	match	<u>watch</u>
5 charm	farm	harm	<u>warm</u>
6 cart	dart	part	<u>wart</u>
7 bull	<u>dull</u>	full	pull
8 could	<u>mould</u>	should	would
9 lint	mint	<u>pint</u>	tint

Unit 12

1
1 don't have to
2 mustn't
3 mustn't need'nt
3 doesn't have to
5 mustn't
6 don't have to need'nt
7 doesn't have to need'nt
8 mustn't

2
1 arrived, was having
2 was driving, had
3 ended, made
4 was lying, went
5 was *still* ringing, got there
6 was living, got
7 became, won
8 took, were sitting

3
1 it had broken
2 I'd/had built
3 we'd/had bought
4 he'd/had caught
5 she'd/had chosen
6 they'd/had cost
7 you'd/had drunk
8 she'd/had driven
9 I'd/had eaten
10 you'd/had fallen
11 I'd/had flown
12 she'd/had forgotten
13 I'd/had given
14 he'd/had grown
15 I'd/had heard
16 it had hurt
17 we'd/had met
18 I'd/had rung
19 it had shone
20 they'd/had slept
21 I'd/had stood
22 we'd/had swum
23 she'd/had taught
24 I'd/had thought

4
1 'd/had been
2 had begun
3 'd/had started
4 was
5 decided
6 'd/had wandered
7 saw
8 said
9 looked
10 went
11 asked
12 said
13 'd/had been
14 liked
15 'd/had worked
16 knew
17 was
18 asked
19 'd/had done
20 liked
21 cooked
22 came
23 left
24 stayed
25 got
26 'd/had met
27 forgot
28 thought
29 was
30 decided

5 1 B, 2 B, 3 C, 4 C, 5 B

6
1 had climbed   were driving
2 had left
3 was trying   had taken   hadn't found
4 had become   was holding
5 had won   had sunk   had tied

7
1 can
2 must
3 can
4 have to
5 may
6 must
7 can
8 can
9 should
10 can

8
camera(wo)man	film director
chef	waiter/waitress
computer programmer	software designer
detective	police(wo)man
editor	reporter
flight attendant	pilot
interpreter	translator
judge	lawyer
model	photographer
nun	priest

Answers

10
1. ~~ties~~ toys
2. ~~tape~~ type
3. ~~hoses~~ houses
4. ~~pie~~ pay
5. ~~couch~~ coach
6. ~~boy~~ buy
7. ~~lines~~ lanes
8. ~~pails~~ piles
9. ~~bound~~ boned

Unit 13

1
1. seeing
2. to hear
3. to use
4. missing
5. getting
6. to want
7. investing
8. to hire
9. discussing
10. to have

2
1. finish
2. seems
3. ask
4. avoid
5. appears
6. offer
7. keeps
8. wants

3
1. to want to find
2. agreeing to do
3. trying to like
4. to ask to go
5. to avoid doing
6. to expect to earn

4
1. to post
2. to pass
3. hitting
4. moving
5. leaving
6. to become
7. to see
8. to visit

5
1. to say
2. leaving
3. playing
4. to hand in
5. to bring
6. to stop
7. working
8. risking

6
1. trying to lose
2. forgot meeting
3. tried cycling
4. went on to start
5. stopped to have
6. regret calling
7. like to see
8. remember telling, mean to say

7
1. ahead
2. over
3. about
4. away with
5. along
6. at
7. back to
8. down to
9. by

8
taxi driver
police officer
school teacher
mechanical engineer
registered nurse
kitchen porter
refuse collector
sous chef
university lecturer
marketing executive
motor mechanic
nursing auxiliary
civil servant
computer programmer

10
1. more
2. far
3. bore
4. sir
5. here
6. near
7. there
8. care
9. heart
10. farm
11. short
12. born
13. earth
14. word

Unit 14

1
1 e 2 d 3 a 4 g 5 f 6 b 7 c

2
1. used to
2. used to
3. 's used to
4. used to
5. 's getting used to
6. get used to
7. used to
8. getting used to
9. 'm used to
10. didn't use to

3
1. My car was hit by a truck.
2. This work is now done by machines.
3. Your computer was fixed.
4. The new hospital was opened by the Health Minister.
5. A new process was invented last year.
6. The book was taken from my bag.
7. You are asked not to smoke in here.
8. Her brother has been arrested by the police.
9. The interview was filmed for the 6 o'clock news.
10. Is Irish still spoken?

Answers

4 1 a 2 a 3 b 4 a 5 b 6 b 7 a 8 b

5
1 issued
2 appointed
3 employed
4 notified
5 recognised
6 provided

6
1 been
2 be
3 have
4 are being
5 be
6 have
7 be
8 been

7
1 sets in
2 set upon
3 set aside
4 setting up
5 set about
6 set off

8 dog   donkey   bone   Nice   cut   dirty   day's   short   down

10

•••	••••	•••	••••
Fung's not here.	Write a letter.	*Bob needs a break.*	It's not my job.
Pay them now.	Adam likes you.	Where do you work?	The boss is mad.
Where's her desk?	Help me print it.	Send him a text.	He's gone to France.

Unit 15

1
1 If you give me the data I'll/will write the report
2 If the rain stops we'll/will go to the park
3 I'll/will give Mr Hassan the information if I see him.
4 If I have enough money I'll/will buy a new jacket
5 If Naria needs books she'll/will get them from the library
6 You'll/will enjoy that course if you take it.
7 If you fill in this form I'll/will process your application
8 I'll/will go for a swim if I have time tomorrow

2 1 g 2 d 3 h 4 i 5 f 6 c 7 a 8 b 9 e

3
1 When   leave
2 if   give
3 when   comes
4 If   pass
5 If   throw
6 try   if
7 have   when
8 When   ends

4 1 g 2 i 3 h 4 e 5 d 6 j 7 b 8 c 9 a 10 f

5
1 He's been watching me for ten minutes.
2 She's been crying.
3 I've been waiting for ten minutes.
4 He's been fighting.
5 They've been travelling since yesterday morning.
6 Mark's been sleeping (on the couch) for two hours.
7 I've been reading this book for a month.
8 I've been speaking to the boss about this for weeks.

6
1 lived
2 been telling
3 arrived
4 worked
5 been crying
6 dropped
7 scored
8 been fighting
9 been sending

7
1 get
2 will/'ll speak
3 goes, finish
4 leave, will/'ll go
5 will/'ll wait, ends
6 will/'ll go, arrive
7 loves, will/'ll live, dies
8 finishes, will/'ll go

8 1 e 10 d 2 f 6 c 5 g 7 b 9 a 8 i 3 h

9
1 put in for
2 put on
3 put up
4 put across
5 put out
6 put off
7 put by
8 put forward
9 put up with

10 b e a j d f k i h g c

11 1 j 2 h 3 i 4 d 5 b 6 c 7 l 8 a 9 k 10 g 11 f 12 e

Unit 16

1
1 had/would help
2 'd/would get   did
3 was/were   'd/would speak
4 'd/would buy   had
5 wouldn't take   was/were
6 drove   'd/would go
7 'd/would earn   did
8 stopped   'd/would

2
1 knew   'd/would tell
2 finish   'll/will call
3 was/were   'd/would be
4 was/were   'd/would invest
5 see   will you give
6 was/were   'd/would fix
7 win   'll/will share
8 has   'll/will help

81

Answers

3
1. had
2. was
3. goes
4. is
5. rains
6. was
7. was
8. is
9. was
10. see

4
1. If Bridget were here she'd/would help us.
2. If I were a cat I'd/would chase mice.
3. If I were as rich as my uncle I'd/would live in a big house.
4. If it were possible we'd/would do it.
5. If I were tall I'd/would play basketball.
6. If he were good at the job we'd/would keep him on.

5
1. got
2. to know
3. knew
4. took (though *take* is possible)
5. sees
6. had
7. go to see
8. didn't go
9. knew
10. finishes answering to come see

6
1. would
2. might
3. might
4. could
5. could
6. Could
7. might
8. would
9. could

7
1. up
2. in
3. for
4. after
5. around
6. at
7. back

8
1. luggage
2. boot
3. pavement
4. garden
5. holiday
6. trouser
7. windscreen
8. autumn
9. bonnet
10. tyres
11. junction
12. motorway
13. lever
14. queue
15. aeroplane

10

1.

dʒ	ɪ	ɒ	g	r	ə	f	ɪ
h	b	aɪ	ɒ	l	ə	dʒ	ɪ
ɪ	ɪ	m	j	ʊ	z	ɪ	k
s	ŋ	f	r	e	n	ʃ	m
t	g	d	ɑ	ɑ	m	ə	æ
ə	l	dʒ	ɜː	m	ə	n	θ
r	ɪ	s	aɪ	ə	n	s	s
ɪ	ʃ	f	ɪ	z	ɪ	k	s

across

geography
biology
music
French
drama
science
physics

down

history
English
maths

ESOL
for Scottish Qualifications
WORKBOOK

ESOL for Scottish Qualifications will help students to prepare for SQA assessments in English for Speakers of Other Languages at Access 3 and Intermediate 1 levels and provides a basis for future success in SQA/ESOL examinations. The essential skills of reading, writing, listening and speaking are covered, plus the key elements of grammar and pronunciation. It offers full coverage of the Transactional, Everyday Communication and Work and Study modules and tasks are clearly differentiated as Core or Extension to enable usage with multi-level classes. This accompanying Workbook provides a range of consolidation and practice exercises to support the learning activities which the Student's Book contains.

Also available:
ESOL for Scottish Qualifications Student's Book: 978 0 340 97138 3
ESOL for Scottish Qualifications Teacher's Book: 978 0 340 97305 9

Hodder Gibson
Educational Publishers for Scotland

At Hodder Gibson we offer a wide variety of textbooks and revision guides aimed specifically at the Scottish examination system. Please contact us for details of other titles at hoddergibson@hodder.co.uk, tel 0141 848 1609, or write to us at 2A Christie Street, Paisley PA1 1NB.

This workbook is endorsed by the Scottish Qualifications Authority

www.hoddergibson.co.uk

ISBN 978-0-340-97139-0